SATURATION
BIBLE STUDY

SATURATION BIBLE STUDY

THE ADVENTURE TO KNOW JESUS
AND BE TRANSFORMED BY TRUTH

NR JOHNSON

Deeper Christian Press
Christ-Centered Teaching and Resources

SATURATION BIBLE STUDY
the adventure to know Jesus and be transformed by truth

© 2023 by NRJohnson
Published by Deeper Christian Press | Windsor, Colorado

Paperback ISBN: 978-1-953549-06-8
EBook ISBN:978-1-953549-07-5

Cover photo © by Kevin Carden / Lightstock

· · · · ·

· · · · ·

deeperChristian.com
This ministry is maintained by the Lord
through the stewardship of those who value it.

CONTENTS

PART 2: THE PROCESS OF BIBLE STUDY

APPENDIX

FOREWARD

Eric Ludy

To study the Bible is the world's greatest task. It is, in one way, easier than learning to crawl, and yet, in another way, more difficult than climbing Mt. Everest.

To truly know God through the Scriptures is an achievement far greater than Michaelangelo's painting of the Sistine Chapel — it is an epic venture that will demand extreme perseverance, dauntless faith, and great humility. And yet, it doesn't take a doctoral degree to pull this off. This tremendous achievement could be accomplished by even a child — if that child hungers and thirsts for it.

The Heavens are watching with bated breath to see who will be the next great pursuer of God Almighty via His Word. So few that possess this grand book, known as the Bible, actually study it, immerse themselves in its Truth, and saturate themselves in its majestic message. Instead, they tip-toe along its Gospel pathway and strategically pluck the flowers of forgiveness, redemption, and grace in order to make a beautiful, soul-pacifying bouquet for the kitchen counter of the soul.

What they pluck *is* Truth and the bouquet they look upon *is* wonderful. But, though it is true and wonderful, it is a scant loveliness compared to the boundless beauty planted in the garden of God's great revelation. There is so much more to explore. There is real intimacy with God to gain. And so few actually explore this heavenly Garden, allowing the Holy Spirit to show them the countless exquisite pathways of intimacy that lie hidden around every turn in the Garden's Gospel pathway.

This book is a tour guide of God's grand Garden of Truth. It is an intimate brush with the power and beauty of the Scriptures. It is a wonderful showcase of the Person of Jesus Christ, and how to discover Him more and more in and through the study of the Bible.

Nathan Johnson is the rare sort of man that has spent his life climbing this Scriptural Everest, painting this wondrous Sistine Chapel, and exploring the beauty and power of this Gospel Garden. When Nathan teaches his Saturation Bible Study at Ellerslie, it is like a field trip to the botanical gardens of heaven — the fragrance of Christ wafts throughout the Chapel building and literally stuns the students with its divine loveliness.

The reason you hold this book in your hand right now is likely because you, too, desire to be one of the few in this generation that genuinely and passionately pursues the Person of Jesus Christ through the pages of Scripture. I can think of no better way to begin that epic journey than by reading this book.

Of course, this book is *not* the Bible. But it is like a dear friend, ready to take you by the hand, and fearlessly and confidently lead you *into* the Bible.

Cheering you on down the Narrow Way of the Cross!
— Eric Ludy
Bestselling author, international speaker,
and president of Ellerslie Mission Society

THE IMPORTANCE OF SATURATION

Stephen Manley

As a sophomore in high school, I struggled with Christianity. My teenage battle was not about information or understanding but commitment and a sense of reality. I was conflicted by the pull of the world, which was really about doing my own thing against the call of Christ. One day during my lunch hour, I slipped across the street to the church. I was alone in a Sunday school classroom without the stimulus of gospel music or the emotion of an appealing altar call. The challenge was simple. Either Christianity works, or it does not. Either the presence of Jesus is real, or He is not. In complete commitment to Jesus, I dared Him to be real in my life, or I was going to look elsewhere for my life's purpose.

I saw no lightning bolts or felt any strong emotions, which may have been a part of my problem. I had been looking for such a manifestation. As I made my way back to the high school, I did not feel any different. However, for months something or Someone began to happen within me! I had a growing awareness that Jesus Himself, the real person of Jesus, was living within my flesh. Another person besides myself had come to live within my body. Jesus' Spirit merged with my life. His mind and my mind, His heart and my heart, His emotions and my emotions became one.

In this merger, I became aware of the possibility of what I later called "saturation." I could saturate in His presence all the time. I could live in a "God-awareness." I could be in constant communication with the Lover of my soul. It became the norm for me to walk the halls of the high school, aware of His presence. In my mind, I called Jesus front and center for every problem. The consistent sharing of every life experience became my constant delight. The challenge of changing from "I" language to "we" language was essential because this new creature is not "I" and "Him" but "us!"

Jesus brought to my attention a little book entitled, **The Practice of the Presence of God.** The author, Brother Lawrence, was a monk in a monastery whose responsibility was to work in the kitchen. He wrote to a friend that his superiors required much time praying at the altar, but he found no difference between the altar and the kitchen. Communication with Jesus was the same in both places. Paul proclaimed, "Pray without ceasing" (1 Thessalonians 5:17). The Greek word **adialeiptos**, translated as "without ceasing," is an adverb describing and giving content to the imperative verb, "Pray." "Without ceasing" means "unremittingly, incessantly, permanently, continually, without intermission." Prayer is the atmosphere in which the merger between man and God occurs, a communication level and state of existence of the "new creature."

A new approach to the Scriptures suddenly appeared. I desperately wanted Him to be a part of the communication as I saturated in His presence. I found the Living Word began to communicate through the Written Word. The Scriptures became more than academic writings; the voice of Jesus sounded in my heart through the Scriptures. Saturating in the Scriptures stimulated a new depth in saturating in His presence. The Scriptures became a living organism of His presence in my life. I was no longer merely having devotions or meeting a requirement, but Jesus was revealing Himself through the Scriptures.

I want this for you as well. May this book on Saturation Bible Study open up for you a greater intimacy with Jesus through His Word.

What a journey!

— Dr. Stephen Manley
Itinerant evangelist, author of more than 50 books,
and founder of Cross Style Ministries

PART 1

THE PURPOSE OF BIBLE STUDY

1

THE ADVENTURE OF A LIFETIME

The invitation to a journey guaranteed to change your life

The vigor of our spiritual life will be in exact proportion to the place held by the Bible in our life and thoughts. I solemnly state this from the experience of 54 years. The first three years after conversion I neglected the word of God. Since I began to search it diligently the blessing has been wonderful. Great has been the blessing from consecutive, diligent, daily study. I look upon it as a lost day when I have not had a good time over the word of God.
George Müller

Welcome to the adventure of a lifetime!

When you begin an adventure, you hazard unknown difficulties and dare to laugh in the face of danger...all the while knowing the reward is well worth the risk.

Some people seek adventure by climbing Everest or

jumping from a plane. Others paddle down class five rapids or take an arctic plunge in mid-January. Some take an ancient ring and travel across dangerous lands to throw it into a volcano, while others just want to read about it.

Yet all these adventures fall short of the greatest adventure of all time — knowing the God of the Universe.

Missionary and martyr Jim Elliot once said, "Oh, the fullness, pleasure, sheer excitement of knowing God on earth!"[1]

Nothing compares to actually knowing God Almighty. Many of us know facts, details, and information **about** Him, but too few of us truly know Him.

This book is an invitation (and practical guide) to know the Living God through His Word. The goal isn't to gain more information but to grow in intimacy.

AN INVITATION TO INTIMACY

Perhaps like no other time in history, humans today have more competition for their time, attention, and affection. Our focus is lured away like a kid in a candy store from the source of life — God Himself.

This has been the ploy of the enemy from the beginning. In Eden, the serpent enticed Eve to turn her trust and focus from God toward herself. By eating the forbidden fruit, she declared she wanted to be the judge between good and evil. She wanted to be independent of God. Her gaze turned from the Creator to the creation. Humanity sinned and lost its intimacy with God. Yet God relentlessly pursued His people.

Throughout Scripture, God beckons His bride to "repent" and "return." He longs for us to leave our idolatrous affair with the world and pursue Him alone.

He wants relationship with us, offering us everything we need for life and godliness (see 2 Peter 1:3). Yet we are a distracted people, often wanting God to be an "add-on" to our lives rather than be at the center.

Yet our heart's longing is for Him. The cry within our soul tells us there is more to be discovered in Christ — more joy, more peace, more victory, more hope, more life, and more intimacy. As such, we have a nagging sense that we should spend more time in His Word and prayer. But we tell ourselves we are either too busy or don't know how.

I grew up in church. Week after week, I heard how important the Bible was to the Christian life, but the problem was no one taught me how to study it.

I read the Bible a few times during my teen years, hoping it would suffice. I asked people around me how they studied, but it was little more than reading. I read a couple of books on the topic. But sadly, my time in Scripture became a duty, an obligation to prove my spirituality.

I didn't delight in God's Word. I mainly wanted to check it off my to-do list; I did it because I was supposed to.

Can you relate?

At age 22, I spent my summer traveling with an itinerant evangelist named Stephen Manley, who later became a dear friend and mentor. During the first week, Stephen sat me down and told me something which caused a dramatic shift in my engagement with God's Word — something that has never allowed me to remain the same. He simply said:

"Reading and studying the Bible shouldn't be for academic study, but for intimacy."

Up till then, I had come to the Bible for many reasons: for devotions, leisure reading, to prove someone wrong, for homework, and to academically know what it means. But in the end, I had missed the true purpose of Bible reading and study.

That summer, I began to shift the focus of why I spent time in Scripture, and everything in my life began to change. Seriously, I do mean everything.

- I began to experience an intimacy and oneness with Jesus I didn't know was possible.

- I started to gain victory over sin.

- My relationships with others improved.

- I had a deep passion to pour my life out and serve the Lord.

- The fruit of the Spirit began to grow in my life — for the first time, I began to walk in an increasing reality of love, joy, peace, patience, kindness, goodness, faithfulness, gentleness, and self-control, as Galatians 5:22–23 talks about.

My world turned upside-down. So much so, at the end of the summer, I told Stephen I was frustrated with him because he "ruined my life." I would never be able to be the same again. I was ruined; in the best possible way.

I look back over the last two decades and I am baffled at the amazing transformation God has done in my life. What began as an invitation to know and experience God through His Word has become one of the most exciting things in my life. Not only did I discover how the Christian life actually works, but Jesus, through His Word, has radically changed every aspect of my life — spiritual, physical, mental, emotional, and relational.

I can boldly proclaim with Paul in 2 Corinthians 5:17 that I am a new creation in Christ Jesus — the old has passed away, behold the new has come!

What caused the dramatic change in my life? It was the transforming work of Christ as I drew in intimacy with Him through His Word.

Stephen taught me the importance of "why" I should study Scripture (intimacy with Jesus) and introduced me to the concept of Saturation — which has forever changed how I approach God's Word.

For the past two decades, I have taught thousands of other believers Saturation Bible Study and have seen countless lives transformed by the truth of Scripture. And I want you to experience the same freedom, life, and transformation.

So I invite you on a journey, an adventure guaranteed to change your life. We may not climb Everest or raft down a treacherous river together, but this adventure will be more breathtaking, exhilarating, and certainly far more fun.

> **The men that have been the most heroic for God have had the greatest devotional lives.**
> Leonard Ravenhill

I want to guide you down a path that will set you free to read and study the Bible with greater joy, passion, and understanding. An adventure to know Jesus and be transformed by truth.

Let's dive in!

2

KNOWING JESUS

The difference between knowing and knowing about

*In the deep recesses of man's soul lies
an overwhelming yearning toward the
Creator. This is a common thread through
all humanity, created in the image of God.
Unless and until that desire is fully met,
the human soul remains restless,
constantly striving for that which
is ultimately unattainable.*
A.W. Tozer

*Ignorance of the Scripture
is ignorance of Christ.*
Jerome of Stridon

I love a good cookbook.

I have a dozen picture-filled volumes on my bookshelf that make my eyes bulge and mouth water. Occasionally, I will pull one out and flip through the pages until I find something that looks delightfully delicious. I stare at the pictures, read through the ingredients, and imagine how amazing it must taste. But I soon put the book back on my shelf and go about my life, never tasting the delectable goodness.

Many of us do the same thing, not just with God's Word, but with God Himself.

We attend church, ooh and aah in praise, pull out our "biblical cookbook" and read some passages, we smile and nod at how amazing God is...only to return Him to the bookshelf of our lives and return to normal living. If we are more serious, we may memorize the ingredient list and cooking instructions of His Word, even producing articles or podcasts about the goodness of the groceries.

We may know all about God and His Word, but have we actually tasted and seen that the LORD is good? Psalm 34:8 exhorts us, "O taste and see that the LORD is good; How blessed is the man who takes refuge in Him!"

> **You don't need to [merely] know the word of God; you need to know the God of the word.**
>
> Leonard Ravenhill

The difference between knowing information *about* God and truly knowing Him is as different as knowing the details of a recipe and delighting in the mouthwatering dish.

Knowing about God *is* important, but knowing and experiencing Him through relationship and intimacy is even more essential.

KNOWING KNOWLEDGE

The Greek word *ginsokō* contains a concept that has radically changed my life.

Various words are translated as "knowledge" in biblical Greek (what the New Testament was written in). One gives the idea of knowing something through facts, data, and information — like the knowledge you gain from reading a newspaper or textbook. Another suggests perception and insight, usually associated with sight (we say, "oh, I see it!" meaning we have gained mental clarity on a topic). And then there's the word ginōskō.

Ginōskō knows something through experience or relationship. This word has a variety of uses throughout the Bible, but the basic idea is that you learn about and understand something because you have spent time experiencing it. This goes beyond textbook comprehension or being told information; ginōskō is not about academics but a relational understanding.

There is a vast difference between:

- studying the technique of how to swim and jumping into a pool

- seeing the speed limit sign and experiencing the law by being pulled over

- watching a documentary of the Grand Canyon and standing on the edge, awestruck at the landscape

- knowing the ingredients of a recipe and tasting the meal

As you spend time and experience life with someone, the relationship becomes more robust, and you know them more deeply. Yes, you learn more *about* them, but the time together also allows you to know them at a level far beyond information or academics. It's relational, intimate, and experiential. That's the idea behind ginōskō.

Have you ever seen a cute old couple? I love cute

old couples. Have you ever been around a couple married for over fifty years? A couple who has spent that much time together knows each other so well they often have their own unique language. They use words, phrases, and facial expressions to communicate with each other in ways others may not understand; they just know what each other is thinking. Couples with fifty years of life experience and relationship together often know each other so well that they talk, act, and even start to look like each other. That is a ginōskō type of knowledge.

Imagine having that level of depth and intimacy with Jesus.

This type of intimacy between you and God is defined as eternal life. In John 17:3, Jesus said, "This is eternal life, that they may know [ginōskō] You, the only true God, and Jesus Christ whom You have sent." Jesus said eternal life is knowing Him intimately and deeply. Eternal life isn't learning *about* Jesus; it is having a relationship with Him.

You can know all the facts, details, and information about God; you can go to church, read your Bible, pray, and tithe; but none of these give you eternal life. Eternal life is knowing Jesus — actually knowing Him — getting wrapped up in relationship and intimacy with the God of the universe.

What if you had the same type of relationship with Jesus that a cute old couple experiences — a relationship where the more time you spend with Him, the more you think like Him, talk like Him, act like Him, and even start to look like Him?

We'd have to call you a Christian.

GINŌSKŌ IN THE WORD

Many believers approach Scripture desirous for more information — details, stories, and facts. They treat the Bible like a cookbook, reading recipes and investigating ingredients. They close the Book knowing more about God but having spent little to no time with Him.

Academic knowledge of the Bible isn't bad. We *should* learn the information and details of God's Word. We should plow its depths and understand the intricacies of Scripture. But our desire to know more about the Bible shouldn't surpass our longing to know God Himself. Information is good, but intimacy is better.

Just as there is a significant difference between staring at a picture of the ocean and wading in its waves, there is a difference between reading and studying the Bible for academics and experiencing the truth of Scripture.

Many scholars and students use the Bible in classroom discussion and study (both in Christian and secular schools). They analyze the words, they debate the meaning, but in the end, they may have excellent head knowledge, but little to nothing in their lives have changed. They may know a lot about the Word, but they haven't experienced the transformation and impact the Word is to produce in us.

> **When the child of God**
> **Looks into the Word of God**
> **And sees the Son of God**
> **He is changed by**
> **the Spirit of God**
> **Into the image of God**
> **For the glory of God**
> Warren Wiersbe

We will discuss this more in chapter 6, but suffice it to say, it is possible to read and study the Bible and never encounter God. Again, knowing information, academics, and details isn't wrong; they just can't save or transform a life. They can point us toward the solution (Jesus), but we need a relationship — an intimate knowing — with Christ Jesus. The academics are to merely facilitate and lead us toward a greater ginōskō with Jesus.

We live in what many historians call the "information age" — a time marked by increased information. We are enamored by the latest tidbit, allured by new research, and geek out over new and improved ways of doing something. Even in the Church, information and academics have become a primary focus for many believers. And while we need to study biblically, I encourage you to come to Scripture with the desire to deepen your relationship and intimacy with God.

Yes, I keep repeating myself — and I do so because we so often ignore this key truth with Bible study — we must have intimacy over academics. Transformation is ultimately more important than information.

Saturation Bible Study will teach you how to study so you can ginōskō Jesus — know Him more, love Him more, experience Him more, and grow more in your relationship with Him.

But if you desire to ginōskō Jesus, you first need to understand the importance of spiritual heartburn.

———

Dive Deeper

verb

1) To go below the surface
and explore greater depths.

2) Questions and exercises to help you think
through and apply the concepts of the chapter.

3) A practical guide to growing spiritually and
deeply knowing [ginōskō] Jesus and His Word.

———

DIVE DEEPER

- Define the term ginōskō in your own words and explain why it's essential in Bible study.

- Why is intimacy with God more important than information about Him?

- Spend time in prayer and ask God for a greater longing for Him.

- Consider taking the concept of ginōskō even deeper by checking out my book *Knowing Jesus*.

3

YOU NEED SPIRITUAL HEARTBURN

Experience the joy, power, and transformation of God's Word

When our quiet times have become hurried, how can we expect to give God the adoration that is His due? How can we receive the guidance that God is waiting to give? How can our hearts catch the glow of divine fire? How can we have deep fellowship with those purposes that are really nearest to the heart of God?
Gordon M. Guinness

I've never experienced a heart attack, but I've always wanted to...spiritually, that is. Most people who have had a heart attack never remain the same; it changes them and how they live. I want that transforming experience in my spiritual life.

Perhaps "heart attack" seems too intense, so let's talk about heartburn. Physical heartburn occurs in some people as a burning sensation in the chest after eating certain kinds of food. And while this pain is often undesired and medicated, spiritual heartburn should be sought after and treasured.

One of my favorite passages of Scripture deals with the reality of spiritual heartburn.

Luke records the encounter of two disciples with Jesus after His crucifixion and resurrection. As these two disciples walked the seven miles from Jerusalem to a small town called Emmaus, they talked about the crucifixion of Jesus, the one they thought was the Messiah. I imagine their grief and confusion were overwhelming.

During their journey, Jesus — whom they did not recognize (see Luke 24:16) — interrupted their discussion and asked about their conversation and why they were downcast.

Cleopas, taken aback, responded, "Are You the only one visiting Jerusalem and unaware of the things which have happened here in these days?" (Luke 24:18).

Upon further question, Cleopas explained the previous day's events, ending with the devastation that their savior, the Messiah, had died (see Luke 24:19–24).

Jesus gave a rebuke, and "beginning with Moses and with all the prophets, He explained to them the things concerning Himself in all the Scriptures" (Luke 24:27).

Over the next several miles, Jesus walked through the Old Testament, showcasing Himself in each passage. For example, while we don't know what specific passages He used, He may have brought up the fact that He is:

- The Creator of the universe (Genesis 1–2)
- The seed of the woman (Genesis 3:14–15)
- The second Adam (Genesis 3:6)

- The Tree of Life (Genesis 3:23–24)
- The ark of deliverance that saves from judgment (Genesis 6)
- The Passover Lamb (Exodus 12)
- The manna and rock in the wilderness (Exodus 16–17)
- The Suffering Servant (Isaiah 53)[2]

Regardless of the specific passages Jesus used, the afternoon walk was full of wondrous illustrations of how Christ is revealed on every page of Scripture.

Arriving in town, they encouraged Jesus (whom they had still not recognized) to stay with them and have dinner as the day was approaching sundown. As Jesus took the bread and pronounced a blessing, the eyes of the two disciples were opened, and they saw it was Jesus who journeyed with them.

As Jesus vanished out of sight, they said to each other, "Were not our hearts burning within us while He was speaking to us on the road, while He was explaining the Scriptures to us?" (Luke 24:32).

Reread the passage. They experienced spiritual heartburn as Jesus revealed Himself through the Word!

And like the disciples on the road to Emmaus, when you open God's Word and encounter Jesus, you will experience spiritual heartburn — a searing awakening in your heart that produces greater passion, love, and longing for Him.

He is the one that produces the spiritual heartburn; it can't be manufactured or stirred up by yourself. Heartburn comes as the Holy Spirit reveals Jesus to us, primarily through Scripture.[3] Jesus said to His disciples,

> "But when He, the Spirit of truth, comes, He will guide you into all the truth; for He will not speak on His own initiative, but whatever He hears, He will speak; and He will disclose to you what is to come. He will glorify Me, for He will take of Mine and will disclose it to you" (John 16:13–14).

The Holy Spirit guides us into Jesus (who is the truth, see John 14:6). So as we come to God's Word, the Holy Spirit discloses, guides, glorifies, and ultimately reveals Jesus to us, which results in spiritual heartburn.

THE TREE IN THE MIDST OF THE WATER

I long to live with perpetual spiritual heartburn. And while I'm not there yet, one of the easiest ways for me to burn is to be in God's Word.

I love when God reveals Himself to me through His Word. For example, Exodus 15:22–26 deeply stirs me.

> Then Moses led Israel from the Red Sea, and they went out into the wilderness of Shur; and they went three days in the wilderness and found no water. When they came to Marah, they could not drink the waters of Marah, for they were bitter; therefore it was named Marah. So the people grumbled at Moses, saying, "What shall we drink?" Then he cried out to the LORD, and the LORD showed him a tree; and he threw it into the waters, and the waters became sweet.... [And God said], "for I, the LORD, am your healer."

The Israelites were desperate for water and had gone too far to turn around. They came to a pool, but the water was polluted and bitter. So God provided a solution: a tree. When Moses threw the tree into the pool, the water not only became clean, it was made sweet. And God revealed one of His names: Jehovah Rapha (the God that heals you).

While this seems like a random account in the life of ancient Israel, it's also our story. While it is true and historical, it is also a foreshadow pointing to the greater reality of Jesus Christ and the power of the Gospel. Let me explain.

Our lives are bitter and polluted because of sin, and they are not as they should be. Paul describes our lives before Christ this way:

> "And you were dead in your trespasses and sins, in which you formerly walked according to the course of this world, according to the prince of the power of the air, of the spirit that is now working in the sons of disobedience. Among them we too all formerly lived in the lusts of our flesh, indulging the desires of the flesh and of the mind, and were by nature children of wrath, even as the rest" (Ephesians 2:1–3).

Our lives are polluted with sin, impurity, and indulgence of every kind. The waters of our souls are undrinkable and bitter. We need the Gospel!

Paul continues with the two amazing words "But God" — "But God, being rich in mercy, because of His great love with which He loved us, even when we were dead in our transgressions, made us alive together with Christ (by grace you have been saved)" (Ephesians 2:4–5). Our salvation was purchased by Jesus dying upon a tree.

Let's go back to Moses. The Israelites were dying of thirst, and there was no hope, only bitter water. Yet, when a tree was thrown into the midst of the polluted water, it was transformed into something not merely clean but also sweet. So too, in our lives. When the Cross of Christ is planted in the midst of our sin and polluted lives, He makes us clean and full of life. We are transformed by the power of the Cross and the effectual working of the Gospel. God is Jehovah Rapha in my life — He turns the bitter waters of my soul sweet.

What a phenomenal truth!

Such truth causes me to stand in awe and wonder of our King. I marvel at how God reveals Himself and the Gospel upon every page of Scripture. And it profoundly stirs my soul; it creates heartburn to know Him more, love Him more, and delight in Him more.

I love the lyrics to the song *Know You More* by Steve Green. The chorus says:

> Oh, I want to know You more, deep within my soul I want to know you. Oh, I want to know You, to feel your heart and know Your mind. Looking in Your eyes, stirs up within me. Cries that say, "I want to know You, oh, I want to know You, more"

Do you desire God like that? Reading about the similarities between the Israelites and your own life, did you experience a flicker of passion and heartburn realizing that while you don't deserve it, Christ died for you, planting a tree in the midst of your bitter-polluted waters creating a new life marked by purity and sweetness?!

That's what God's Word does. It not only teaches us about who our amazing God is and all He has done, but the Word also stirs our hearts and transforms our lives.

While we may not experience a burning within the heart everytime we come to Scripture, we should long for it. We should ask God to reveal Himself to us through His Word.

Let's do that now. Pray with me.

> *Lord Jesus, it is You I desire to encounter in Your Word. Teach me Your Word, but in doing so, stir within me a passion for truth, a longing for*

a greater relationship, and increase my awe and wonder of who You are. Breathe upon my soul and give me spiritual heartburn that continues and increases over time. Lord, I want to know You, not just more facts about You. May the reward of my diligent seeking after You be a greater relationship with You. In Your precious Name I pray. Amen.

DIVE DEEPER

- Have you ever read the Bible and experienced "spiritual heartburn"? If so, what was it that stirred your heart? How would you describe spiritual heartburn from your experience?

- Do you desire to experience spiritual heartburn, why or why not?

4

HOW TO BREATHE WATER

Discover the heart of Saturation

Remember that it is not a hasty reading, but serious meditation on holy and heavenly truths, that makes them prove sweet and profitable to the soul. It is not the mere touching of the flower by the bee that gathers honey, but her abiding for a time on the flower that draws out the sweet. It is not he that reads most, but he that meditates most, that will prove to be the choicest, sweetest, wisest and strongest Christian.
Thomas Brooks

Have you ever marinated meat?

You take raw meat, toss it in a marinade, and let it soak. After a couple of hours, you find that the meat has been transformed. Somehow the marinade has infused itself into the meat and made it even more delicious.

Or perhaps you've used a French Press to make coffee.

Rather than filter the coffee, you put the grounds right into the water, allowing the beans and water to come together, and later press out the grounds to leave amazing coffee.

Take the idea of marinade or French Press coffee and bring it to your engagement with the Bible.

Many of us think of our time in the Bible as a checklist item. We spend fifteen minutes reading or studying the Bible, check it off the list, and move on to the next thing for the day. But God longs to have more than a head nod toward His Word each morning.

> **He that would be holy must steep himself in the Word, must bask in the sunshine which radiates from each page of revelation.**
>
> Horatius Bonar

Imagine a sponge in a bucket of water. Every pore and crevice of the sponge is full of liquid. The sponge is consumed with and defined by the water contained within. We would look at the sponge and say it is soaked, saturated, and permeated with water.

What if you could be that way with Scripture?

What if you were a sponge plunged into a bucket of water called the Word? What if your entire life was filled, saturated, and consumed with His truth?

Saturation.

As a basic definition, **saturation** is the idea of filling something to its fullness — to absorb a substance to the fullest extent.

Many people read and study their Bibles with a "how much do I have to do to please God" mentality, but what if our focus wasn't on how little we can get by with, but how filled can we be? What if our goal wasn't "a chapter a day to keep the devil away" but becoming consumed and obsessed with God and His Word?

Just as you marinate meat to transform the taste or make coffee with a French Press to heighten its flavor, we saturate in God's Word to deepen our intimacy and enrich our relationship with Jesus Christ.

SCRIPTURE SATURATION

So what does it mean to saturate in God's Word?

Let's go back to a simple definition: saturation is filling up and absorbing something to the fullest extent — in our case, Scripture. The concept of Saturation Bible Study is taking the Bible and bringing it into our lives throughout the day. Rather than spend a few minutes reading or studying the Bible in the morning, bring the study with you and ponder it all day long.

Growing up in church, I was told to read my Bible. So I'd read a chapter or two and go about my day. But once I learned about saturation, I would take what I've read and continue to think about it throughout the day.

God told Joshua, "This book of the law shall not depart from your mouth, but you shall *meditate on it day and night*, so that you may be careful to do according to all that is written in it; for then you will make your way prosperous, and then you will have success" (Joshua 1:8).

> **Reading the Bible without meditating on it is like trying to eat without swallowing.**
> Anonymous

The concept of meditation has been hijacked and perverted by the modern New Age movement, where it has become an activity where you empty your mind. But biblically, meditation is about filling up your mind with truth and reflecting upon it. You've probably heard the common illustration that biblical meditation is like a cow chewing its cud. A cow eats grass, swallows, and later brings it back up to chew on it some more. Over and over, it regurgitates its food to continue chewing on it. That's how we should meditate upon God's Word — eat, swallow, and bring it back up to chew (ponder and reflect) upon it throughout the day.

Psalm 1:2 reminds us that a person is blessed when their "delight is in the law of the LORD, and in His law he *meditates day and night.*" In the Psalms, the phrase "the law" can either refer to the Law of Moses or the entirety of Scripture. In either case, it should be our delight to meditate upon God's Word day and night.

We are told several times in Psalm 119, a psalm all about the beauty and delight of God's Word, that you should delight and meditate upon God's ways, precepts, and promises (see verses 6, 15–16, 24, 27, 35, 47–48, 70, 77–78, 92, 97, 143, 148, 174).

Solomon said we are to take the wise words and "Do not let them depart from your sight; keep them in the midst of your heart" (Proverbs 4:21).

In summary, Scripture urges us to take God's Word and hide it in our hearts, delight in it, remember it, and meditate upon it throughout the day and night. To use one word, we are to **saturate**. Like a sponge filled with water, we need to fill up our lives with the Word of God and be consumed, permeated, and saturated with truth.

Before I give you some practical ideas on how to saturate in God's Word, let me give you another illustration.

BREATHING WATER

Imagine being on a boat off the coast of Australia on the Great Barrier Reef. If you look down into the water, you may get excited to see a few fish near the boat. But if you never get out of the boat, put on a snorkel mask, and get your face in the water, you'd miss a world of beauty.

Sitting on the boat isn't bad, but it isn't nearly as impressive as having your face in the water. Yet you could go even further by donning scuba gear and spending time in the depths. Just as you see more with a snorkel mask than staying topside on the boat, you see much more with scuba gear when you spend extended time below the surface.

For the sake of illustration, imagine if you could grow gills and live in the water. Life in the water would unveil even greater insights, beauty, and wonders than scuba gear ever could give you.

Now apply this simple illustration to Bible study. When you read the Bible, it is similar to sitting on the deck of a boat looking down into the waters of the Word. Sure, you will discover things, but you're missing a lot by not getting your face into it. While you should read the Bible, you also need to get out of the boat and dive into the water.

As you memorize and meditate upon Scripture, it's like putting on a snorkel mask. Scuba gear is similar to most people's study habits as they spend time in the depths. But saturating is like growing gills and living in the Word.

ABIDING IN THE WORD

To change the illustration, think of a tree. The life sap of the tree flows up through the trunk into its branches. If a branch desires to receive the life of the tree and produce fruit, it must hold tight to and abide in the trunk of the tree. The tree is the only source of life for a branch.

Jesus explained this concept to His disciples by talking about the vine and branches. In John 15:1–5, Jesus said,

> "I am the true vine, and My Father is the vine-grower. Every branch in Me that does not bear fruit, He takes away; and every branch that bears fruit, He cleans [prunes] it so that it may bear more fruit. You are already clean because of the word which I have spoken to you. Abide in Me, and I in you. As the branch cannot bear fruit from itself unless it abides in the vine, so neither can you unless you abide in Me. I am the vine, you are the branches; he who abides in Me and I in him, he bears much fruit, for apart from Me you can do nothing" (LSB).

Branches that do not bear fruit are dead and must be cut off, and branches that are alive and producing fruit need to be pruned. While it appears the job description of a branch is to bear fruit, the fruit is actually a byproduct, a natural result, of abiding. When a branch abides, it receives the life of the vine and *will* produce fruit. Thus the focus and work of a branch is not on producing fruit but on maintaining the abiding relationship with the source of life.

I love the concept of abiding. The Greek word for abide is *menō*, meaning "to remain, stay, reside, sink down into, hold tight to." But my favorite definition is "to refuse to depart." A branch must "refuse to depart" from the life of the vine. A branch doesn't vacation in the vine, nor does it spend fifteen minutes each day abiding and then does its own thing. Such activity is death for the branch. A branch, to be alive, must remain connected to the life of the vine; it must refuse to depart.

So too, I must "refuse to depart" from the life of Jesus. He alone is my source of life, for He is life itself (see John 14:6, Galatians 2:20, Philippians 1:21, and Colossians 3:4).

Jesus used the same concept for your involvement in His Word: "So Jesus said to the Jews who had believed him, 'If you abide in my word, you are truly my disciples, and you will know the truth, and the truth will set you free'" (John 8:31–32 ESV).

Just as we abide in Christ Jesus for life, we must also abide in His Word. We must cling to, refuse to depart from, and rest in the Word of truth. We cannot give lip service and declare we are a Christian (a disciple of Christ) if we are not living in and from His Word.

Saturation is a lot like abiding. A branch must continually abide in the life of the vine — it needs to be saturated (filled up to the fullest extent) with the life-giving sap which produces fruit through it. When we saturate, we abide in God's Word and allow it to invade and fill up every part of our lives. We must "refuse to depart" from Scripture and continually bring our hearts and minds back into a focus upon and agreement with God's Word.

We can't casually engage with the Word; we must live in it. This isn't a devotional vacation spot we visit once a year, once a month, or even once a week. It should be our daily food and nourishment. Just as the Israelites in the wilderness had to gather manna daily to survive, so too we must abide in God's Word daily. Moses reminded the Israelites,

> "He humbled you and let you be hungry, and fed you with manna which you did not know, nor did your fathers know, that He might make you understand that man does not live by bread alone, but man lives by everything that proceeds out of the mouth of the LORD" (Deuteronomy 8:3).

Note the purpose of the manna — it wasn't just to feed their bellies but to teach them that they didn't live by physical food but by the Word of God. This is still true for us today.

Like a sponge in water or a branch abiding in the vine, we need to saturate ourselves in the Word of God and allow it to permeate and infiltrate every aspect of our lives.

4 WAYS TO SATUATE IN SCRIPTURE RIGHT NOW

Saturation is not so much a "method" of how to study as much as it is a concept that affects all of your time in Scripture. In section two of this book, I will give you a process for how to study the Bible, but whether you read, memorize, meditate, or study, you can saturate in God's Word — which means you can begin to saturate in Scripture right now. Here are four suggestions.

1. READ AND REFLECT

Take something you've read in Scripture recently and think about it throughout the day. In the random spare moments of the day (driving, waiting in line, brushing your teeth, etc.), think about what the passage means and why God put it in His Word. How can you apply this Scripture to your life today?

2. LISTEN AND LEARN

Instead of turning on the tunes, consider listening to an audio Bible. When you drive across town, get ready in the morning, or wind down at the end of the day, listening to the Bible is a great way to fill up your mind with truth. You may not catch everything said, but you'll be surprised at how much listening to Scripture over and over will affect the way you think, talk, and live.

3. MEMORIZE AND MULL OVER

Memorizing Scripture is a wonderful way to fill your mind with the Word. When you memorize, you must ponder and recite the passage often to keep it engrained in your mind. Consider taking a longer passage (like Psalm 23, 1 Corinthians 13, or the book of Colossians) and begin to memorize it. Start with one verse and keep adding verses until you're able to quote the entire passage; then, review it often so you don't forget it.

4. DIG DEEP AND DISCOVER

Start with a single verse and write it on a notecard. Carry the notecard with you wherever you go throughout the day; in spare moments, reread the verse and consider what it means. Choose one of the main words and look up what it means in light of the passage and the surrounding verses. This is similar to the "read and reflect" above but intentionally goes deeper into the meaning of words, ideas, etc. Use the back of the card to write down thoughts, ideas, and other things you may want to look up when you have additional time.

Again the idea, whether you read, study, memorize, or listen to God's Word, is to soak and saturate in it — to ponder it throughout the day, allow it to fill up your life, and live according to the truth.

My best saturation times have happened while I brush my teeth, mow the lawn, or drive across town — because I allow the Word to percolate, soak, and marinate in my life. And as I abide in the Word, it radically changes how I think, feel, see, talk, and live. My life bears fruit not because I grit my teeth trying to produce it but because I refuse to depart from the life of Christ and His fruit is the natural byproduct.

As you build your life around God and His Word, you'll discover that your time in the Word will transition from a checklist activity you do for a few minutes each day to a time of intimacy and communion with God all throughout the day.

So let's become like a sponge in a bucket of water and be soaked, saturated, and permeated with Scripture. But our desire for saturation must be based on two key reasons why we should study the Bible. Let's talk about those next.

> **The man who would truly know God must give time to Him.**
>
> A.W. Tozer

DIVE DEEPER

Take our passage from John 15 and ponder it throughout today.

> "I am the true vine, and My Father is the vine-grower. Every branch in Me that does not bear fruit, He takes away; and every branch that bears fruit, He cleans [prunes] it so that it may bear more fruit. You are already clean because of the word which I have spoken to you. Abide in Me, and I in you. As the branch cannot bear fruit from itself unless it abides in the vine, so neither can you unless you abide in Me. I am the vine, you are the branches; he who abides in Me and I in him, he bears much fruit, for apart from Me you can do nothing" (John 15:1–5, LSB).

Consider asking yourself these questions as you reflect upon it:

- Why does the vinedresser delight in pruning branches?

- What is the focus of a branch?

- Why is "abiding" so important and repeated in this passage?

- How is fruit a result of abiding rather than self-effort?

- How would you summarize what Jesus is saying in a single statement?

5

IT'S ALL ABOUT TWO REASONS

Remove every other motive why you read and study the Bible

The more you love the Scriptures, the firmer will be your faith. There is little backsliding when people love the Scriptures.
D.L. Moody

The most important and profitable time of my whole day is the time I spend with God.
Andrew Murray

I used to read a lot of books on health and weight loss. I knew facts, details, and concepts about becoming strong and healthy. I could impress you with big terms, a passionate speech, and an outline of crucial workouts and diets. But my life didn't reflect it; I was unhealthy.

Though I spent years wishing my health would improve and my weight would decrease, it wasn't until I finally realized that health is more than information;

it required a change of lifestyle. I knew it to be true in my mind, but it was merely head knowledge — facts and details from a book.

Many Christians have head knowledge about the Bible and even know how to study, but they don't do it. Like reading books on health but never eating right or exercising, if we know HOW to do something without knowing the WHY behind it, our motivation will wane, we quickly become frustrated, and too often, we stop altogether.

Knowing HOW to do something doesn't change our lives. All of us know how to do a lot of things, but our lives aren't affected or different. If we want our lives to be different, we must first know the WHY.

In my journey toward health, it was only when I understood WHY I needed to be healthy that the HOW finally made sense, and my life began to change. I have been able to triumph through the grueling workouts and the not-so-fun eating plans (i.e., the HOW) because I have a firm grasp on my WHY.

The same is true regarding our interaction with the Bible. Too few Christians see the benefit or connection between the Bible and their everyday lives. They know they should read and study the Bible, but it's intimidating — a big book written in an entirely different culture than they have experienced. It takes a lot of time to read and do the work of studying it. So why do it?

SEVEN PROBLEM REASONS

Over the years, I've noticed people typically come to Scripture for at least one of the seven reasons.

1. PRESSURE

Many believers feel pressure to be in the Word if they want to be a "good Christian." They feel guilty if they don't open the Bible. For preachers and teachers, there is an added pressure to be in the Word to prepare messages.

2. PROVING

Some people come to Scripture to find evidence that supports their conclusions to prove a point or win an argument. They use the Bible as a weapon of destruction to prove someone wrong rather than as a tool to share the Gospel.

3. PARTICULARS

Many Christians come to the Bible in search of information, not transformation. Their motives may vary, but the purpose is to understand the particulars and gain head knowledge. Their focus is absorbed with details, information, education, and facts.

4. PLEASURE

Other people read the Bible for pure enjoyment or entertainment. It is leisure reading. The danger is they can see God's Word as nothing more than good moral stories or amusing fictional accounts.

5. PERFORMANCE

When I was in seminary, I had a lot of homework using the Bible, and grades were based on my performance and time in the Word. The same mentality seeps in with the need to check off "devotions" from our daily to-do list. It becomes a duty rather than a delight, a "have to" rather than a "get to." In short, our time in the Bible can be all about performance.

6. PROBATION

Many Christians feel the need to win God's approval and favor. They believe God will give them a good day if they read their Bibles and a bad day if they don't. But this is not God's heart or nature. He does not send people to probation based on their time in the Word. Similar to "performance," people with a probation mentality try to win God's affirmation and are often marked by tremendous guilt, obligation, and pressure.

7. PSYCHICAL

The least popular (hopefully) for genuine believers is the psychical or paranormal approach to the Bible which sees it as a good-luck charm, a rabbit's foot, or something that will "ward off demons by flicking its pages."

THE TWO PRIMARY REASONS FOR STUDYING SCRIPTURE

Each of these seven reasons has problems and dangers associated with them. As such, would you be willing to lay down every reason you've come to the Bible in the past and embrace a new way of thinking? I want to introduce you to the two primary reasons you should dive into the Bible.

1. INTIMACY

The main purpose for getting into God's Word is to know Jesus.

We've already discussed the Greek word *ginōskō* (see chapter 2). As a refresher, the word is typically used to describe knowing something through experience or relationship. Ginōskō goes beyond head knowledge into an interactive-experiential type of knowing.

While academics, details, and information are not bad, the focus of Bible study is Jesus Christ. As the Author of Scripture, we must seek to know Him, not just information about Him.

I briefly told you about my time with Stephen Manley in the summer of 2005 when he taught me the basics of Saturation Bible Study. Though it may appear subtle, the shift from academics to intimacy with the Author was radical in my life. It not only created a greater hunger and passion for God and His Word, but I better understood the depths of Scripture. My time in Scripture drew me into a continual encounter with the Living God, and my life has never been the same.

Since that summer, I have found, like King David, that God's Word is more "desirable than gold, yes, than much fine gold; sweeter also than honey and the drippings of the honeycomb" (Psalm 19:10). The Bible has become a pure-sweet delight, and I wouldn't trade anything for the relationship I have with Jesus because of my time spent growing in His Word.

I now dive into the pages of Scripture (both the Old and New Testaments) to know Christ. I don't merely want to know information about Him; I want to know Him intimately.

When we study God's Word, our desire must go beyond academics to seek intimacy with the Living God. Academics aren't bad; knowing the stories, learning facts, and understanding what a passage means are all beneficial. But we engage with the Word of God to discover who He is, encounter His life, and deepen our relationship with

Him. Just as we spend time with a best friend to deepen and enrich the friendship, we also need to spend time in God's Word to grow in intimacy and know His heart, mind, and life.

> **The end of all learning is to know God, and out of that knowledge to love and imitate Him.**
>
> John Milton

You have the privilege of privileges to know the Creator of the universe — for He has made Himself known. He has revealed Himself not through static text but through His Word, which is living and active. The primary reason we should be in Scripture is to know the Author.

2. TRANSFORMATION

The result of knowing Jesus is a transformed life.

As I experience God and intimately know Him through His Word, He will change my life. The writer of Hebrews reminds us that the Word of God:

> is living and active and sharper than any two-edged sword, and piercing as far as the division of soul and spirit, of both joints and marrow, and able to judge the thoughts and intentions of the heart (Hebrews 4:12).

As we interact with God's Word, our lives are confronted by the truth, measured against the perfect standard of Scripture, and we are transformed. Like a hot stove or a fire that burns the hand upon touch, as we respond to the truth God reveals in His Word, He radically changes our thinking, actions, speech, motives, attitudes, and desires. His desire is to conform us to the image of Christ.

We all know Paul's famous passage in Romans 8:28, "And we know that all things work together for good to those who love God, to those who are the called according to His purpose" (NKJV). But we often stop there and forget the purpose is found in verse 29: "For those whom He foreknew, He also predestined to **become conformed to the image of His Son**, so that He would be the firstborn among many brethren." God's desire is for us to become conformed to the image of Jesus.

Do you remember playing with Play-doh and plastic molds? You take one of the fun plastic molds shaped like some animal and you shove the Play-doh inside, removing everything that doesn't fit. That's the concept of "conforming" — God uses "all things" in our lives (the good, bad, and ugly) to shove us into a mold shaped in the image of Christ. Anything in our lives which doesn't look like Him He removes (we call this sanctification).

When you believe and put your faith in Christ, He changes your life so significantly that the New Testament declares you a "brand new creature" or "creation" (see 2 Corinthians 5:17). As the first creation recorded in Genesis 1–2 was a picture of radical transformation, God has also changed your life from darkness to light and from death to life. But He isn't finished with you; you still need God's sanctifying work to cleanse, change, and continue shaping you into the image of Christ. And His primary sanctifying tool is Scripture: "Sanctify them [purify, consecrate, separate them for Yourself, make them holy] by the Truth; Your Word is Truth" (John 17:17, AMP).

The more we study God's Word, the more the Holy Spirit will expose what needs to change in our lives. He will use the Word as a magnifying glass and a measuring tape to reveal the truth to show us what holy, righteous, godly living looks like...and where our lives don't measure up.

The more we get to know Jesus through His Word, the more we are acquainted with the "plastic mold" He is conforming us to. And as we see the discrepancy between our current lives and the life of Christ, it should cause a longing for transformation and repentance. After Peter preached at Pentecost, those who heard were "pierced to the heart, and said to Peter and the rest of the apostles, 'Brethren, what shall we do?'" (Acts 2:37). Peter told them to repent and be baptized. As we repent and respond to God's work in our lives, we will experience continual sanctification and transformation. Like a sharp sword, God's Word will cut and change our lives when we embrace it.

See the progression: as I come to the Bible to know the Author (Jesus), experience His life, and grow in relationship and intimacy with Him, He will transform my life with truth.

There are numerous benefits to studying the Bible, but the two primary reasons to come to Scripture are to know Jesus and, as an outflow, to be transformed by truth.

In the coming chapters, we will talk more about how this happens and how to do it. But to experience life change through God's Word, we need to talk about the proper posture you need when coming to Scripture. Let's dive into that next.

See Appendix 3 for eleven amazing blessings and benefits you receive when you read and study the Bible.

6

THE PROPER POSTURE

5 things your life must be marked by to get the most from your study

And the Bible itself, though it is nourishment, though it is light, though it is warmth, though it is medicine to the soul, yet it never helps anybody where there is not serious attention given to it.
A.W. Tozer

I never saw a fruit-bearing Christian who was not a student of the Bible.
D.L. Moody

Anyone can pick up the Bible and get something out of it. Christians, non-believers, intellectuals, simpletons, everyone.

And because God uses His Word in the lives of unbelievers to bring conviction and stir them to repentance and salvation, we need to share God's Word with others — it is powerful, effective, and as Paul reminds us:

> For "everyone who calls on the name of the Lord will be saved." How then will they call on him in whom they have not believed? And how are they to believe in him of whom they have never heard? And how are they to hear without someone preaching? And how are they to preach unless they are sent? As it is written, "How beautiful are the feet of those who preach the good news!" But they have not all obeyed the gospel. For Isaiah says, "Lord, who has believed what he has heard from us?" So faith comes from hearing, and hearing through the word of Christ (Romans 10:13–17, ESV).

But just because someone can read and learn from the Bible doesn't mean they are students of Scripture. The Bible is not a textbook to glean information from; it is a spiritual and supernatural book that demands something from its readers.

As a Christian, if you desire to understand the Bible and be transformed by truth, you must come to Scripture with these five marks in your life:

1. Holy Spirit
2. Belief
3. Humility
4. Obedience (unto holiness)
5. Undistracted Devotion (focus)

Let's look at each one in detail.

YOUR LIFE MUST BE MARKED BY
1. THE HOLY SPIRIT

An unbeliever can study Scripture academically, but only a Christian with a new heart can truly see and understand the things of God. This is because you cannot know God solely through research and mere information. You may discover facts about Him, but true biblical insight and revelation are given by the Holy Spirit and experienced through a relationship with Him. An unrepentant and unbelieving heart won't be able to properly understand the truth, no matter how smart the mind is.

The Bible is a spiritual book; it contains the very words of God. Thus you need more than human reasoning or intellect to grasp its meaning.

A good illustration is found in Acts 4:13. The religious leaders "observed the confidence of Peter and John and understood that they were uneducated and untrained men, they were amazed, and began to recognize them as having been with Jesus." The power of the disciples' preaching wasn't because of human wisdom or education but because they spent time with Jesus and were filled with His Spirit.

After Jesus fed the 5000, He said to His disciples, "...the words that I have spoken to you are spirit and are life" (John 6:63b). While this was true of everything He said while on earth, it is also true of His Word from Genesis through Revelation. The nature of Scripture is spiritual, and thus we need to be Spirit-filled to understand it properly.

The Christian life isn't segmented into areas that are spiritual and others that are secular. You don't live a divided life. Everything you do is to be worship unto the glory of God (see 1 Corinthians 10:31 and Colossians 3:17). And as Jesus told the Samaritan woman at the well, "God is spirit, and those who worship Him must worship in spirit and truth" (John 4:24). Everything, including your reading and study of Scripture, is worship and should be done in spirit and truth.

YOU NEED THE SPIRIT OF GOD

Though the disciples had been with Jesus for three years, they were told to wait for the Holy Spirit, which Jesus called "The Promise of the Father" (see Luke 24:49, Acts 1:4–5, 2:33). It was only after Pentecost, the outpouring of the Holy Spirit, that the world was turned upside down because of their witness in Jerusalem, Judea, Samaria, and the ends of the earth. Without the Holy Spirit, their self-effort, talent, and wisdom were insufficient. They needed God's power, providence, and presence in their lives through the indwelling Holy Spirit. And if the disciples who traveled and talked face-to-face with Jesus needed the Holy Spirit, how much more do we need Him?

The Promise of the Father wasn't reserved only for the disciples but for everyone who puts their faith in the Lord Jesus. As Peter explained in his sermon on Pentecost, "For the promise is for you and your children and for all who are far off, as many as the Lord our God will call to Himself" (Acts 2:39). You are included! The Holy Spirit isn't an add-on to the Christian life; He is the very source of that life.

Paul prayed the Ephesians would "**know** (ginōskō) the love of Christ which surpasses **knowledge**, that you may be filled up to all the fullness of God" (Ephesians 3:19). Paul uses two different words for knowledge — the first is an intimate and experiential form of knowing (ginōskō), which he says surpasses an academic knowledge and understanding of Christ's love. In other words, we can have information about the love of Christ, but to experience it is far superior. The same is true with all of Scripture — we may have academic awareness yet never embrace or experience its transforming truth.

We must "know" the Word, which surpasses academic "knowledge" of it.

This experiential revelation of Scripture is given by the Holy Spirit. Jesus told His disciples in John 16:13, "But when He, the Spirit of truth, comes, He will guide you into all the truth; for He will not speak on His own initiative, but whatever He hears, He will speak; and He will disclose to you what is to come." Paul said the same thing when he prayed "that the God of our Lord Jesus Christ, the Father of glory, may give you the Spirit of wisdom and of revelation in the knowledge of Him..." (Ephesians 1:17 ESV).

Without the Holy Spirit, the Bible remains a mystery. Even Jews, the people of God, don't have a full grasp of the Old Testament without the illumination of the Spirit. In 2 Corinthians 3, Paul uses an illustration comparing the veil which covered the face of Moses when he came down the mountain of God (see Exodus 34:29–35) to the veil which covers the face of Israelites when they read Scripture. Paul writes,

> **The Bible without the Holy Spirit is a sundial by moonlight.**
> D.L. Moody

> Therefore having such a hope, we use great boldness in our speech, and are not like Moses, who used to put a veil over his face so that the sons of Israel would not look intently at the end of what was fading away. But their minds were hardened; for until this very day at the reading of the old covenant the same veil remains unlifted, because it is removed in Christ. But to this day whenever Moses is read, a veil lies over their heart; but whenever a person turns to the Lord, the veil is taken away. Now the Lord is the Spirit, and where the Spirit of the Lord is, there is liberty. But we all, with unveiled face, beholding as in a mirror the

glory of the Lord, are being transformed into the same image from glory to glory, just as from the Lord, the Spirit (2 Corinthians 3:12–18).

Without seeing Scripture in light of Jesus Christ and being freed from the veil through the Spirit, the Jews miss the whole point of the Bible. They may read the words, but their understanding of the Word is cloaked. The same is true with all of us — we need the Holy Spirit to bring divine insight and understanding of the Word.

In his first letter to the Corinthians, Paul explains that God reveals His mystery and wisdom to us through His indwelling Spirit.

> …but we speak God's wisdom in a mystery, the hidden wisdom which God predestined before the ages to our glory; the wisdom which none of the rulers of this age has understood; for if they had understood it they would not have crucified the Lord of glory; but just as it is written, "THINGS WHICH EYE HAS NOT SEEN AND EAR HAS NOT HEARD, AND which HAVE NOT ENTERED THE HEART OF MAN, ALL THAT GOD HAS PREPARED FOR THOSE WHO LOVE HIM." For to us God revealed them through the Spirit; for the Spirit searches all things, even the depths of God. For who among men knows the thoughts of a man except the spirit of the man which is in him? Even so the thoughts of God no one knows except the Spirit of God. Now we have received, not the spirit of the world, but the Spirit who is from God, so that we may know the things freely given to us by God, which things we also speak, not in words taught by human wisdom, but in those taught by the Spirit, combining spiritual thoughts with spiritual words. But a natural man does not accept the things of the Spirit of God, for they are foolishness to him; and he cannot understand them, because they are spiritually appraised (1 Corinthians 2:7–14).

Go back and reread the passage. Notice how often it mentions the concept that God reveals His truth to us through His Spirit.

Again, God's mysteries, wisdom, and revelation are revealed and taught by the Spirit. And Paul makes an important point, the natural man (an unbeliever) is unable to understand the things of God — and counts them as foolishness — because he is unspiritual. The flesh (the selfish, carnal, sinful nature) wants nothing to do with God because the flesh is hostile to the Spirit. As Paul reminds us in Romans 8:5–10,

> For those who live according to the flesh set their minds on the things of the flesh, but those who live according to the Spirit set their minds on the things of the Spirit. For to set the mind on the flesh is death, but to set the mind on the Spirit is life and peace. For the mind that is set on the flesh is hostile to God, for it does not submit to God's law; indeed, it cannot. Those who are in the flesh cannot please God. You, however, are not in the flesh but in the Spirit, if in fact the Spirit of God dwells in you. Anyone who does not have the Spirit of Christ does not belong to him. But if Christ is in you, although the body is dead because of sin, the Spirit is life because of righteousness (ESV).

Martin Luther explained it this way, "Man is like a pillar of salt, he's like Lot's wife, he's like a log or a stone, he's like a lifeless statue which uses neither eyes nor mouth, neither sense nor heart until that man is converted and regenerated by the Holy Spirit. And until that happens, man will never know God's truth."[4]

So let's recap. To properly understand God's Word, you

> **The Bible is a supernatural book and can be understood only by supernatural aid.**
>
> A.W. Tozer

must be a Christian — someone who has put their faith in the Lord Jesus has a regenerated heart and life, and has the Holy Spirit within.

The Bible is spiritual, so we must be Spirit-filled.

YOUR LIFE MUST BE MARKED BY
2. BELIEF

Entire books have been written about the validity and truthfulness of Scripture. But even more than being factually true, which it is, Jesus called His Word *the truth* (see John 17:17).

Truth demands a response. You cannot be passive when you encounter truth — you either must agree and submit to it or find a way to silence it.

If Scripture is the truth, the question that confronts our lives is, will we believe it?

The word "believe," which is found nearly a hundred times in the Gospel of John, is the theme and purpose of his book (see John 20:30–31). We often think of belief as a mental grasp of something, but that misses its emphasis. In the Greek New Testament, *belief* and *faith* come from the same root word. To believe *(pisteuō)* is a verb (an action) and faith *(pistis)* is a noun. When you have faith, it means you're doing the action of believing; likewise, when you believe, we call that faith. This is why we are called believers — the people of faith.

But again, belief is more than mental assent or a concept to understand intellectually. Let me give you my favorite illustration.

Imagine I take you up in an airplane and open the side door to show you the incredible view. As you look at the landscape below, I come behind you and give you a push. Upon hearing your scream, I realize you might need a parachute, so I find one and throw it out the door toward you. I then yell from the plane, "Do you believe in the parachute?"

You see it falling above you and respond above the howling wind, "Yes! I believe!"

But seeing the parachute and having the mental belief in its ability will not help you. To believe, in this illustration, is to somehow make your way over to the parachute, put it on, and hang on for dear life. The parachute is your sole means of salvation, which you must wear to enjoy its saving benefit.

Likewise, to believe in the Lord Jesus isn't to have a mental understanding of Him; even the demons have an intellectual knowledge and shudder (see James 2:19), but they aren't saved. To believe (have faith), you must put on the Lord Jesus Christ (see Romans 13:14 and Ephesians 2:8) and hold tight to Him, for He is your sole means of life and salvation.

We need to move beyond hearing God's Word but doing nothing about it — and instead, come under its authority, obey, and put it into action. Our trust, hope, faith, and obedience to God's Word comes from an active belief in it. Read through Hebrews 11 afresh and see how these ordinary men and women are commended for their faith in and obedience to what God said (i.e., His Word).

Genuine belief in the truth will alter your attitude and actions. Just as you'd change your nightly walk if you believed a lion escaped the local zoo and was prowling around your neighborhood, so too, believing God's Word will practically change every aspect of your life.

The Bible is the truth, so we must believe.

YOUR LIFE MUST BE MARKED BY
3. HUMILITY

In Appendix 2, I have a section on the supremacy of Scripture. I encourage you to pause this chapter and go read about how the Bible is inerrant (accurate), immutable (unchanging), and infallible (perfect and permanent). The emphasis is that the Bible is to have ultimate authority in our lives. When we approach Scripture, there are only three positions we can take:

1. ABOVE IT

Too many Christians see themselves above God's Word. They scrutinize Scripture according to their opinions or interpretations. If something makes them uncomfortable, they ignore it or explain it away. They take the bait as Eve did in the Garden when the serpent asked, "Did God really say...?"

When you put yourself above Scripture, it no longer has authority in your life, and you stand in a position of pride and arrogance. You attempt to bend the Bible around your life and make it say what you want it to mean. But we cannot be the arbiter of truth — we cannot be the ones who have ultimate authority — that is God's position, and He has given us that truth in His Word.

George Whitefield once declared,

> If we once get above our Bibles, and cease making the written Word of God sole rule both as to faith and practice, we shall soon lie open to all manner of delusion, and be in great danger of making shipwreck of faith and a good conscience. Our blessed Lord, though He had the Spirit of God without measure, yet always was governed by, and fought the devil with, "It is written."[5]

2. ALONGSIDE IT

Other Christians wrap their arms around the Bible and become a buddy with it. It may sound more spiritual than standing above Scripture, but this position also strips the authority of Scripture from our lives.

If a close friend came into your home, walked into your room, and demanded that you clean it, you would likely be offended. They don't have the right (the authority) to command you to clean your room. Friends can give suggestions and encouragement, but they don't have authority in our lives. Similarly, when the Bible is merely a buddy, we may allow it to give us a winsome word or a soft suggestion, but we tend to tone down the commands and exhortations intended to be obeyed.

3. BENEATH IT

The only proper position for a Christian is to come under the authority of the Word in humility. We must bend our knees and say, "Yes, Lord!" Whatever the Word says goes.

Since the Bible contains the very words of God, we must take them seriously. We don't explain away, interpret based on our preferences, or ignore passages. We must hear, understand, and obey what He says. Rather than bend the Bible around our lives, we must allow God to bend our lives around the Bible. If something in us doesn't measure up to His standard, if sin resides, if an attitude or motive is revealed as incorrect, we must allow the transforming work of God's Spirit to change any and everything in our lives so He can make us holy and Christlike.

Are you willing to submit, surrender, and obey God's Word? God will not entrust His treasure to those who don't value it. Unless you are teachable, desirous of truth, and willing to be searched and tried, you will come to Scripture with an arrogant attitude rather than a humble heart. Humility is the posture every believer must have to receive God's Word. As James 1:21b reminds us: "...in humility receive the word implanted, which is able to save your souls."

David wrote in Psalm 139:23, "Search me, O God, and know my heart; try me and know my anxious thoughts..." This is the posture of humility we need when we approach Scripture.

The moment we walk in pride and arrogance, we stand in opposition to God. James writes, "God is opposed to the proud, but gives grace to the humble" (James 4:6b). The word "opposed" means to resist, be hostile toward, or set an army against. When we live with pride, God sets us at arm's length or, perhaps worse, places His army against us. We must not think we can glean insight from His Word when we walk in pride and arrogance; instead, we must "clothe ourselves with humility" (see 1 Peter 5:5 and Jesus' example in Philippians 2:6–8).

Before we open the pages of Scripture, we must pre-decide that God and His Word are correct and true — and in any area where our life, attitude, or beliefs don't measure up, we are wrong and must be changed. It takes tremendous humility, but only the humble experience God's grace (see again James 4:6 and 1 Peter 5:5).

The Bible is authoritative, so we need a posture of humility.

YOUR LIFE MUST BE MARKED BY
4. OBEDIENCE UNTO HOLINESS

It bears repeating that the Bible contains the very words of God. And because He is holy, His Word is holy. And He has called us to walk in ever-increasing holiness.

Holiness has received a bad reputation in our generation, often understood as a boring lifestyle or a list of things we can't do. But biblically, holiness is *always* a good thing. Holiness is not focused on what you don't get to do but upon what you DO get to do — walk in freedom, life, purity, victory, joy, triumph, and experience the very life of Christ.

The word "holy" means to be set apart, different, otherly, or not like the world. When we say God is holy, we declare He is different, unlike, and set apart from the world. And because He is holy, He has called us to be holy (see Leviticus 11:44–45, 1 Peter 1:15–16).

This command to be holy and different from the world around us continues throughout the New Testament. We are to remove our former way of living according to the culture around us and put on the Lord Jesus Christ (for further study, explore Ephesians 4:17–32).

Peter exhorts, "Therefore, putting aside all malice and all deceit and hypocrisy and envy and all slander, like newborn babies, long for the pure milk of the word, so that by it you may grow in respect to salvation" (1 Peter 2:1–2). "Malice" is a general term for all evil, wickedness, and depravity. If we desire the Word and want to grow spiritually (v.2), we must throw off all evil, wickedness, depravity, deceit, hypocrisy, envy, and slander.

James said the same thing, "Therefore, putting aside all filthiness and all that remains of wickedness, in humility receive the word implanted, which is able to save your souls" (James 1:21).

We must walk in holiness, righteousness, and purity in our engagement with Scripture and in all of life. And as we walk in holiness while repenting of and confessing sin, our desire for and growth in the Word will increase.

THE OBEDIENT RESPONSE

So often in the Christian life, the moment we know we should do something, we run off and try to accomplish it in our own strength, wisdom, and ability. But this is counter to Christianity. We do not live the Christian life by our strength or power but through His. And this is true as it relates to obeying God's Word.

We know we should obey God's Word and live a holy life, but too often, in a self-focused "I can do this" attitude, we grit our teeth and attempt to fabricate the Christ-life within. And if you've ever tried this, you know how exhausting and fruitless such a life is. We might be able to mimic godliness for a season, but it never produces a transformed life. Fake-it-till-you-make-it is not how you live the Christian life.

Yes, we are called to obey God's Word and walk in holiness, but not through self-determined effort. Rather, in humility, we must come before God, ask Him for His Spirit to transform our lives, and respond in obedience to His work within us.

I can't produce holiness and godly living through my own effort and ability. Isaiah reminds me that my best attempt at righteous living is filthy rags (see Isaiah 64:6). The only chance I have to be holy is to allow the One who is holy to invade my life and produce His holiness in and through me. I can't be godly on my own; I need God to produce godliness in me through His Spirit.

Major Ian Thomas once said, "It takes God to be a man!

Man, that is, as God intended man to be! God created man to be inhabited by God for God!"[6]

And while God's activity in our lives produces holiness, godliness, purity, and righteousness, we must intentionally align our lives with His truth and walk in obedience. We don't sit around and passively wait for God to change our lives, doing whatever we please until then. Instead, we actively participate and live by His Spirit in obedience to His Word.

Though the concept is a bit abstract, think of it as a dance. In a ballroom dance, the woman does not lead the dance, nor is she passive. She is fully engaged, participating, and active but she's not in charge. She reacts to the movement of the man and responds in kind. The dance is beautiful when the partners don't attempt to do their own thing but rather when one submits to the leading of the other.

Like a woman in a dance, we are to respond to God's leading, direction, and command. He moves us with His Word and wants to lead us into transformation, but we must respond and follow His lead. We are fully active and engaged in the process, but we obey in response to His Word and the movement of His Spirit in our lives.

Psalm 119:105 tells us God's Word "is a lamp to my feet and a light to my path." The more we respond in obedience to the light we are given from the Word, the more we progress down the path of righteousness. Isaiah calls this path "the highway of holiness" (see Isaiah 35:8), and Jesus calls it the narrow way which leads to life (see Matthew 7:13–14). You often only have enough light for the next step, but as you take that step in obedience, another step becomes clear, progress is made, and a holy life is lived.

God wants to use His Word to show us what our lives are supposed to look like and then use it, via the Holy Spirit, as the tool to transform and sanctify us. He longs to reproduce His fruitful life within us. Every benefit and blessing of the Christian life is found in Christ Jesus and through His Spirit's work in us. Listen to a sampling of verses:

> ...for the kingdom of God is not eating and drinking, but righteousness and peace and joy in the Holy Spirit (Romans 14:17)

> Now may the God of hope fill you with all joy and peace in believing, so that you will abound in hope by the power of the Holy Spirit (Romans 15:13).

> But the fruit of the Spirit is love, joy, peace, patience, kindness, goodness, faithfulness, gentleness, self-control; against such things there is no law (Galatians 5:22–23).

> Blessed be the God and Father of our Lord Jesus Christ, who has blessed us with every spiritual blessing in the heavenly places in Christ (Ephesians 1:3).

> ...that you may be filled up to all the fullness of God (Ephesians 3:19b).

> ...until we all attain to the unity of the faith, and of the knowledge of the Son of God, to a mature man, to the measure of the stature which belongs to the fullness of Christ (Ephesians 4:13).

> ...seeing that His divine power has granted to us everything pertaining to life and godliness, through the true knowledge of Him who called us by His own glory and excellence. For by

these He has granted to us His precious and magnificent promises, so that by them you may become partakers of the divine nature, having escaped the corruption that is in the world by lust (2 Peter 1:3–4).

By this, love is perfected with us, so that we may have confidence in the day of judgment; because as He is, so also are we in this world (1 John 4:17).

Everything we need for life and godliness is found in Christ, and it's the Spirit's work in our life which produces holy living. But we must live in response to His Word and His working in our lives. We do not obey out of obligation or duty but

> **Doers of the Word are the best hearers.**
> Thomas Watson

from a heart of love for Him — "By this we know that we love the children of God, when we love God and observe His commandments" (1 John 5:2).

The Bible is holy and transformative, so we need to be marked by obedience unto holiness.

YOUR LIFE MUST BE MARKED BY

5. AN UNDISTRACTED DEVOTION

The Bible is singular in focus: Jesus. Though it contains many sub-characters and themes, everything in the Word draws us to the central point of Christ and the Cross. Everything in the Old Testament leads us to the Cross, and the New Testament flows from this marvelous reality.

Paul declared, "And when I came to you, brethren, I did not come with superiority of speech or of wisdom, proclaiming to you the testimony of God. For I determined to know nothing among you except Jesus Christ, and Him crucified" (1 Corinthians 2:1–2).

He later wrote the Corinthians he was concerned they would be distracted from the simplicity in Christ — "But I am afraid that, as the serpent deceived Eve by his craftiness, your minds will be led astray from the simplicity and purity of devotion to Christ (2 Corinthians 11:3).

Everything in Scripture ultimately leads us to the glorious gospel and the Person of Jesus Christ. And as I have mentioned multiple times, our purpose in coming to Scripture must be to have an undistracted devotion to Jesus Christ.

> **Anything that dims my vision for Christ, or takes away my taste for Bible study, or cramps me in my prayer life, or makes Christian work difficult, is wrong for me; and I must, as a Christian turn away from it.**
>
> J. Wilbur Chapman

When we come to the Word, our goal must be to gain Christ, not grasp more biblical information and facts. Facts don't change our lives; Jesus does. We must remember God rewards those who diligently seek Him (see Hebrews 11:6). We should not pursue the things God can give us; instead, we should pursue Him. He is the goal and focus — so that in everything He might be preeminent and have first place (see Colossians 1:18).

We must go after the WORD (Jesus) to know His Word more. And the opposite is also true: the Word of God in text (the Bible) leads us to the Word of God in Person (Jesus).

We live in a distracted culture. Noise, beeps, and buzzes are constantly drawing our attention. But if we genuinely desire to know God and His Word, we must, as the Psalmist wrote, "Be still (cease striving) and know that I am God" (Psalm 46:10a). We must have an undistracted devotion in our pursuit of God. We must "seek first His kingdom and His righteousness" (Matthew 6:33) and "hunger and thirst for righteousness" (Matthew 5:6). We need to "desire the pure milk of the word, that you may grow thereby" (1 Peter 2:2 NKJV) and realize the infinite value of pursuing the wisdom of the Word (see Job 23:12, Psalm 19:10, and Proverbs 2:1–5). We, like the Bereans in Paul's day, must receive "the word with great eagerness, examining the Scriptures daily to see whether these things were so" (Acts 17:11).

Just as the Bible is singular in its focus, we also must have an undistracted devotion, a singular focus, and a passionate hunger in our pursuit of Christ and His Word.

THE POSTURE OF THE PERSON

We need a correct posture as we approach Scripture. If we desire to experience the depth, wisdom, and life-transforming power of Scripture, our lives must be marked by:

- the Holy Spirit
- belief
- humility
- obedience unto holiness
- and a pursuit of Christ and His Word with an undistracted devotion

We are called to be men and women of the Word, but it demands the correct posture beneath the Word of God.

DIVE DEEPER

This chapter talked about the five things our lives must be marked and filled with as we come to Scripture — the Holy Spirit, belief, humility, obedience unto holiness, and a pursuit of Christ and His Word with an undistracted devotion.

- Which of these five do you struggle with the most? Why?

- Spend time in prayer and ask God to fill your life with these five "marks."

PART 2

THE PROCESS OF BIBLE STUDY

7

STARTING WELL

Good news for nerds
and hyperactives

*The Word of God I think of as a straight
edge, which shows our own crookedness.
We can't really tell how crooked our
thinking is until we line it up with the
straight edge of Scripture.*
Elisabeth Elliot

Have you ever gotten lost on a road trip?

It is difficult to lose our way these days with GPS on our smartphones, but "back in the good old days," you would never head out on a long road trip without a plan and a map. Otherwise, driving from Albuquerque to Albany may find you in Alberta or Alabama.

Plans are helpful, especially in Bible study.

I've met too many people who spend all their time figuring out what to do and where to go rather than actually studying the Bible. They are like a leaf caught in a whirlpool that endlessly swirls around but goes nowhere. I want to help you avoid that frustration.

STUDY IS A PROCESS

Bible study is a learning process, and it takes time. But like most things, the more you do it, the easier it becomes.

When I decided to get healthy, rather than think and talk about it, I bought a gym membership and, with excitement, spent hours the first day beating up my body. The following day, I hobbled onto the scale, but it didn't show any difference despite the agony in my body. I didn't see immediate results from all the time and effort the first day, and it was months before I went back to the gym (a.k.a. the Pain Palace).

Many of us do the same thing with Bible study. We get excited and spend hours studying but then wait weeks or months to do it again. As I later learned in the gym, you make more significant gains and transformation if you go for fifteen minutes every day rather than multiple hours once a month. Then extend into longer sessions over time.

> Nobody ever outgrows Scripture; the book widens and deepens with our years.
>
> Charles Spurgeon

Short, consistent times always beat out longer, sporadic ones.

And like exercise, Bible study takes time to build new habits and skills, it doesn't come automatically; it's a process you must learn.

Have you ever tried to budget your finances? The first month you think you have it figured out, only to realize there is no food money left in your budget (and you still have three more weeks in the month). It often takes a few months to get into the budgeting groove as you figure out how to dial everything in so it works. Bible study is similar in that it may take some time before you feel like you're truly getting it. The key is to stick with it.

One other comparison between study and exercise is helpful to consider — it compounds over time. When I first went to the gym, I had no idea what I was doing. Everything was foreign to me, I felt out of place, and the weight I could barely lift was laughable. But as I stayed consistent, I could lift more and more weight, I enjoyed going, and my workouts became shorter (because I knew what to do and thus spent less time figuring it out). I've found this to be true in Bible study as well.

Bible study is hard work (a labor of love) and will not give its fruit to those who are lazy or complacent in its study. So be diligent and hold tight to God's promise that "He is a rewarder of those who seek Him" (Hebrews 11:6).

TWO MAIN TYPES OF BIBLE STUDY

Though there are different types of Bible studies, almost all of them can be understood within two major categories: the study of passages or the study of topics. Let's briefly look at both.

1. PASSAGES

In a passage study, you study…wait for it…passages. The primary focus is a specific passage (a verse, paragraph, section, etc.). If you want a new vocabulary term, seminaries call this the "pericope" (pronounced per-rick-ah-pee).

As you study the passage, you'll examine specific words (a word study), look into key topics, and seek to understand what the author is saying, in context, to his audience. This is my favorite way to study — taking a longer passage (like an entire chapter) or studying through a whole book of the Bible verse-by-verse or paragraph-by-paragraph. For example, suppose you want to study the book of Philippians. You could study verse-by-verse or paragraph-by-paragraph through the entire book. You could also zoom in on one specific passage and examine the mindset of a Christian, as found in Philippians 4:4–9. Both would be examples of a passage study.

Over the last twenty years of serious Bible study, I've experienced many blessings from a passage study, but here are four key benefits:

- **You study in context.** Perhaps the most significant benefit of a passage study is the blessing of context. When you study topics and bounce around from passage to passage and book to book, you have to stop and figure out the overall context to properly understand the passage (more on context in chapter 9). But in passage studies, you live in the context all the time. Every study reinforces and reminds you of the central context of the book. As such, it speeds up the process and makes studying one degree easier.

- **You study a variety of topics.** When you study a passage, it "forces" you to explore a variety of topics that you may not typically choose for yourself. In a topical study, you tend to select topics you want to study, but when walking through a passage, it causes you to study whatever topics are in the passage. You may not be able to study each topic as in-depth as you can in a dedicated topical study, but you will gain a basic understanding of each topic in light of the context and book you're studying.

- **You better understand the author's point.** As you stay in a single passage or book, it helps you understand what an author is saying to his audience. Rather than pick and choose random verses from what he says, you see the author's flow of thought and argument and why every verse is essential to the author's point.

- **You always know what's next.** You always know what your next study will be since you study the next verse or paragraph and thus don't have to take the time to come up with topics.

2. TOPICS

The aim of a topical study is to discover what the Bible says on a specific topic.

I divide topical studies into four categories:

1. **Themes** — such as money, faith, grace, salvation, persecution, mercy, circumcision, light, etc.

2. **People** — like David, Esther, Baal, Ezekiel, the Moabites, Zuriel, etc.

3. **Places** — locations such as Jericho, Jerusalem, Jabbok, Jaffa, Jordan, Judah, etc.

4. **Things** — like the ark, tabernacle, rainbow, sword, sheep, chrysoprase stone, etc.

While these are not all standard topical groupings, it is easier to put the people, places, and things in this category since we study them in a similar way (*we should have called them "noun" studies*).

For example, if you want to study the topic of love, you'd want to investigate passages like:

Leviticus 19:18
Psalm 91:14
Proverbs 10:12
Proverbs 17:17
Luke 10:27
John 3:16
John 15:13
Romans 13:10
1 Corinthians 13
1 Corinthians 16:14
Galatians 5:14
1 Peter 4:8
1 John 4:8, 16

But since this is such a large topic in Scripture, you may want to narrow your focus down to something more specific like:

- God's love

- Loving God

- Loving others

- Idolatry (loving something more than God)

- The different kinds of love mentioned in Scripture

Topical studies can be a great addition to your study routine as it helps you become laser-focused on "what does God say about _____?" As you look at what all of Scripture says on the topic, you'll begin to understand God's heart and mind on the subject.

The difficulty with topical studies is that you must guard yourself against "ripping out" a single verse without looking at the context (see chapter 9), which leads to a misunderstanding or misinterpretation of the passage itself. As such, if you do a topical study, you may need to take the time to study the surrounding context of each key verse.

But there is tremendous value in studying topics, such as:

- **You choose your own adventure.** Topical studies allow you to choose your own topic and seek out biblical answers to pressing themes or questions you are dealing with right now.

- **You gain a big-picture view.** As you study the topic throughout all of Scripture, you gain a biblical understanding of what God thinks and commands on the topic. This enables you to summarize the topic and better express the concept to others.

- **You stay in tension.** There are many "tensions" in Scripture where there seems to be a contradiction (e.g., wrath vs. love, God's sovereignty vs. man's free will). As you study a topic, you are forced to be faithful to the text of Scripture and wrestle through the tensions. In a topical study, you can't ignore certain passages because they are uncomfortable or seem to contradict your conclusion; you have to come to a biblical understanding of the topic amidst the tensions. And you'll often discover that the truth is often found in the middle of the tension.[7]

- **You discern better.** Knowing what God says about certain topics helps you discern truth biblically rather than be persuaded and pushed around by cultural correctness and worldly wisdom.

THE NERD AND THE HYPERACTIVE

We are all unique, and that makes creating a plan for Bible study a bit tricky. While there are certain elements that should be in all of our study plans (which we will discuss throughout the remainder of the book), not everyone will study the Bible the same way.

I admit I lean more on the nerd side of the spectrum. I love detailed study, looking up words, and trudging through grammar and original languages. But my friend Jeremiah is far more hyperactive. He bounces around and is in the middle of several different things at the same time. Yet he loves Scripture and gleens a lot from it. He just studies differently than I do.

Whether you lean nerd, hyperactive, or find yourself somewhere in-between, you *can* study. You can encounter God through His Word and have your life radically changed by His truth.

In the following chapters, I want to lay a foundation for how to study the Bible, but in chapter 13, I will give a practical plan to study passages, and in chapter 14, a plan for topics. In those chapters, I want to help the nerd, the hyperactive, and those in the middle use what we've talked about to study Scripture, regardless of academic background or personality.

EXPERIENCING GOD

A personal experience is powerful. I can hear about the delight of chocolate cake, but to taste it firsthand is entirely different. We all need to experience the life-changing power of God's Word for ourselves. While we can listen to sermons, read books, and hear about Aunt Susie's stirring salvation story, there is no substitute for a personal encounter with God and His Word.

As A.W. Tozer said, "A right understanding of the Bible opens to us the only path into the presence of God."[8]

It all comes back to the concept of Saturation. The heart and focus of our time in Scripture is to know Jesus and be transformed by truth. This means regardless of our education or personality, we can all study Scripture and enjoy a deeper intimacy with Christ. We just need to know where to start.

THE ORDER IS IMPORTANT

In math, there is an essential order of operations if you want the correct answer. So too, in Bible study.

At the beginning of her classic book on Bible study, *How to Study your Bible*, Kay Arthur gives an excellent example of the Bible study process. She says,

> To thoroughly study [a] frog, you first go to a river or creek bank where frogs live. You watch their eggs hatch and the tadpoles emerge. You see their back and front legs develop and grow, until they look like frogs and leave the water. After observing how the frogs respond to their new life on land, you catch one and observe it more closely. Eventually you take it to the biology lab where you dissect it to see how it looks on the inside. Afterward, you read what other biologists have learned about frogs to see if your conclusions match.
>
> [Bible study] involves the same process: You begin with the Bible, observe it in its environment, and then take it apart so that you understand it firsthand. Then, when you've seen or discovered all you can on your own, you compare your observations with those of godly men and women who have written about the Word down through the ages.[9]

Whether or not you love amphibians, the example is a good illustration of how we engage in Bible study.

In the following several chapters, we will discuss how to study passages. And just as there is a certain order of operations in math, there are four primary steps to study a passage; each step is necessary and in a specific order.

1. Observation

2. Interpretation

3. Connection

4. Application

Create graphic with the word, key question, and the numbered progression

If you try to interpret a passage before observing it, you'll misunderstand the text. If you don't observe and interpret the text, you'll never know what to apply to your life.

Let's dive into step one: how to observe the text.

When learning how to study the Bible, here are a few terms you may come across and their simple definitions:

- **Expositional** – often used with preaching or teaching, exposition is to understand and explain the details of the text, so you know what it means from the context of the original author and audience.

- **Exegesis** – the expositional process of study (using original languages, grammar, word studies, etc.)

where you search for (draw out) the meaning of a passage in its original context. You allow the text to speak for itself without placing upon it your own interpretation, conclusions, or presumptions.

- **Inductive** – similar to the process of exegesis, inductive Bible study examines a text (often by asking questions) with the key purpose of interpreting (understanding) the text and applying it to your life.

- **Pericope** (pronounced per-rick-ah-pee) – a unit of thought, often a single verse or paragraph, that you focus on to study.

———————

8

STEP ONE: WHAT DOES IT SAY?

How to observe a passage

The great need for the saint is to get his brains at work on the Word of God; otherwise he will stagnate, no matter how much he may name the Name of God.
Oswald Chambers

In a classic illustration, a kindergarten teacher brought a goldfish to class and asked her students to describe the fish.

One boy shot his hand up and declared, "It's orange!" A little girl remarked, "It's breathing water." On and on it went.

The next day the teacher gathered the students around the goldfish and asked them to find new observations of their pet. The kids leaned n, scrutinizing the little creature. One girl commented, "There's a little black dot on its right side but not on the left." Another said, "It only swims in circles." And another, "It's like Nemo where the right fin is slightly smaller than its left."

MAKING OBSERVATIONS

There is a profound truth that the more you observe something, the more you understand the thing examined. This is especially true with Scripture. If you desire to know and understand the Word, you must spend the time to examine it.

The first step of the Bible study process is to make observations. Here's the key question: **What does the text say?** And more specifically: **What does the text say in context?**

You don't draw conclusions or try to determine what the text means (yet). You must first look at the text and see what it says.

The best way to record your observations is to use a notebook or a digital device and list everything you see in the text — big, small, complex, basic... everything. A list of bullet points helps you visually see, organize, and make connections within the passage and surrounding context (more on that in the next chapter). Personally, I love recording my observations on my computer because I can easily cut, paste, re-arrange, add extra details, etc., as I work through the passage.

Let's try it. Go grab something to write with. Seriously. I'll wait.

In chapter 4, we broadly examined the familiar passage of the vine and branches in John 15:1–11. Jesus says,

> "I am the true vine, and My Father is the vinedresser. Every branch in Me that does not bear fruit, He takes away; and every branch that bears fruit, He prunes it so that it may bear more fruit. You are already clean because of the word which I have spoken to you. Abide in Me, and I in you. As the branch cannot bear fruit of itself unless it abides in the vine, so neither can you unless you abide in Me.

I am the vine, you are the branches; he who abides in Me and I in him, he bears much fruit, for apart from Me you can do nothing. If anyone does not abide in Me, he is thrown away as a branch and dries up; and they gather them, and cast them into the fire and they are burned. If you abide in Me, and My words abide in you, ask whatever you wish, and it will be done for you. My Father is glorified by this, that you bear much fruit, and so prove to be My disciples. Just as the Father has loved Me, I have also loved you; abide in My love. If you keep My commandments, you will abide in My love; just as I have kept My Father's commandments and abide in His love. These things I have spoken to you so that My joy may be in you, and that your joy may be made full."

Let's practice making observations of verses one and two. Reread those verses (below) and list the things you see in the text. Here are a couple of questions to get you going:

- Who is talking?

- Who are they talking to?

- What imagery is used?

- What is the result if you bear fruit and if you don't?

- Ask the journalist questions: Who? What? When? Where? Why? How?

- What else do you see in the text? What does the text say?

I am the true vine, and My Father is the vinedresser. Every branch in Me that does not bear fruit, He takes away; and every branch that bears fruit, He prunes it so that it may bear more fruit (John 15:1–2).

OBSERVATIONS:

Jesus is speaking
He is speaking to humanity\his followers
A grape vine - imagery
— If we bear fruit we get trimmed for more product-
ivity or if we don't "we" get removed

Now reread verses four and five and make a list of observations you see.

> *Abide in Me, and I in you. As the branch cannot bear fruit of itself unless it abides in the vine, so neither can you unless you abide in Me. I am the vine, you are the branches; he who abides in Me and I in him, he bears much fruit, for apart from Me you can do nothing (John 15:4-5).*

OBSERVATIONS:

We get our life from Jesus - the vine
we are the branches
We are where the fruit grows
But what does abiding mean?

If you haven't taken the time to actually go through the above exercise, pause now and do it. I've read countless books with exercises and prompts, quickly skipping over them to "finish the book" and check it off my list. But if you genuinely desire to know how to study, these simple (and sometimes cheesy) exercises will help. Before you look at my list of observations below, take the necessary time to do the work yourself. Like learning how to swim, there is a vast difference between reading about how to do it and jumping in the water.

How'd you do?

We will continue to discuss how to make good observations, but here is a list of things I observed:

- Who: Jesus is the one talking in the passage

- To Whom: Jesus is talking to His disciples (John 13–15)

- Where/When: in the Upper Room when Jesus shared Passover with His disciples the week of the crucifixion (John 13:1)

- Jesus uses the imagery of vine and branches (agriculture)

- Jesus is the vine (the source of life for a branch) (v1)

- Jesus doesn't merely describe Himself as a vine but the TRUE vine, giving the indication there are false vines (v1)

- The Father is the vinedresser (v1)

- A simple dictionary definition says a vinedresser is someone who prunes, trains, and cultivates vines

- His disciples are the branches (v5)

- Branches that do not bear fruit are removed (v2)

- Branches that bear fruit are pruned (cut back, something removed), so they bear more fruit — a humble decrease before a fruitful increase (v2)

- In both cases, something is taken away (branches with fruit are trimmed; branches with no fruit are removed completely)

- Jesus uses the word "every branch" twice, so no branch is excluded (v2)

- The heart of the vinedresser is to have the branches bear more fruit (v2)

- Abiding is the focus of a branch and a disciple (v4)

- I am to abide in Jesus, and Jesus is to abide in me (v4)

- A branch is unable to bear fruit on its own; it can only produce fruit when it abides in the vine (v4)

- Jesus says no disciple can bear fruit unless they abide in Him (v4)

- The one who abides in Jesus will bear **much** fruit (v5)

- Apart from Jesus (the vine, the source of life) we can do nothing (v5)

- The branch is to bear fruit (v2, 4), but the focus and "job description" of the branch is not trying to produce fruit through self-effort but by abiding in the life of the vine (v4, 5). Thus, bearing fruit is the natural result of a branch abiding in the vine.

You may have noticed many of my observations were restatements of the text. So why write them down? It helps me slow down, see what is happening, and think through the text differently than if I merely read the words on a page. [In fact, while editing this chapter and rereading the observations above, I gained several new observations and insights on this passage].

But working through the list of observations also brought up some questions:

- What kind of vine is it? Does it even matter?

- If "abiding" is so important, what does that mean, what does abiding look like, and how do I do it?

- What does a pruning process look like for a branch (i.e., a disciple)? Does it hurt? Is it worth it?

- What fruit is a disciple to bear? How do they know if they are bearing fruit?

While I may not have the answers to the questions (yet), writing them down helps me process the text and gives direction to what I should search out later in the study.

THE SECRET TO MAKING GOOD OBSERVATIONS

One of the best ways to make good observations is to ask great questions. And one of the best ways to ask great questions is to ask the question behind the question.

In other words, don't stop asking questions.

Usually, the first question we ask doesn't reveal much; it's the second or third question, the drilling down deeper and deeper, where we find the "gold."

For example, a mother asks her child, "How was school today?" "Fine" is the typical response. Did the mother learn anything? Nope. So she keeps asking questions until she draws out a real answer to her question.

In Bible study, it is often essential to keep asking questions until we peel back the layers to sufficiently understand what is happening. Be inquisitive and don't settle for a surface-level answer.

For example, in the story of Jesus feeding the 5000, Mark records, "And He commanded them all to sit down by groups on the green grass" (Mark 6:39). Why was it necessary for Mark to record that the grass was "green"? If we simply conclude he wanted to comment on the color, we will miss an important insight — so we must continue to ask questions. If we do, we discover that grass in the Middle East is only green for a couple of months of the year during the rainy season (November through March[10]), then dies out and becomes brown the rest of the year.

This insight becomes significant a couple of chapters later as Jesus feeds the 4000 and tells them to sit on the "ground" (Mark 8:6). Both locations were considered "desolate" (see 6:35 and 8:4). It is also interesting to note that when Jesus fed the 5000, He fed Jews near the northern shore of the Sea of Galilee, but when He provided bread for the 4000, they were Gentiles (pagans) on the eastern coast of the sea. Looking at both passages, we can conclude that only a few months have passed (from the green grass of springtime to the barren ground of summer or early fall). Yet, the disciples failed to learn the vital lesson that

God provides, and they responded to Jesus with the same desperate and defeated cry (see Mark 6:35–36 and 8:4). So from asking a series of questions, such as

- Why does Mark record the grass is green?

- Is green grass common in Israel? If not, when does green grass appear?

- Since Jesus feeds two groups with loaves and fish, are there any similarities between the ground mentioned in the two passages?

- What was the disciples' response to Jesus' command to feed the people in both instances?

we discover from Mark's comment about "green grass" that it gives insight into the lack of trust and faith the disciples had in the provision and position Jesus possessed. They participated in an incredible miracle in the feeding of the 5000. Yet a couple of months later, they didn't think Jesus could provide so extraordinarily a second time (also see Mark 6:51–52 and 8:13–21). They missed it. And how we often do the same.

This example illustrates that when we believe every word of Scripture is inspired,[11] every word is significant. When you come across a strange detail (like the color of green grass), it's a flashing light that something is probably going on and worth paying attention to. Try to chase down what it means and see if there is any significance to the passage. Countless times in my studies, these seemingly insignificant details have resulted in little epiphanies that give greater insight into the passage. It always stirs my soul and boosts my faith and confidence in the Word when I see God's brilliance by using everything in Scripture to declare truth.

When you ask questions about a passage, search out the answers and keep asking questions. While this could be an endless process, don't settle with the first question. Ask the question behind the question.

If you want help making observations, I've included a list of nearly one hundred questions and things to look for in Appendix 5. As you approach a passage, you can reference this list to help you think it through, ask questions, see it from various angles, and go below the surface.

OBSERVATION TAKES TIME

The observation stage will take the longest time out of the four steps. But until you understand what the passage says (what is going on in the text), there is no way to correctly interpret or apply it to your life.

So, be patient with the process.

Many of us want to get to the "finish line" of study and thus race to find a quick insight. But the purpose of saturating in God's Word is to know the Author and be transformed by truth. If your goal and "destination" is knowing Jesus, and you get to know Him throughout the entire study process, then there is no need to rush to a quick conclusion.

For example, while marriage is the goal of a romantic relationship, there is tremendous benefit in slowing down and enjoying the process of dating and engagement. If a guy suddenly announced he found his future wife three days ago and plans to marry her tomorrow, we'd probably tell him to slow down and get to know her more. "But the purpose of dating is marriage, and I'm ready to cross the line," he retorts. Yet we all know that while marriage may be the purpose and end goal of engagement, there is great value in the process of getting to know someone during that time.

Or, to illustrate it another way, when I was a kid, my parents took my brother and me to Sea World. As soon as the car backed out of the driveway, I asked how long it would take until we started our vacation. They replied, "We *have* started." I failed to realize the holiday didn't begin when we entered the gates of Sea World; instead, it began when the car tires left the neighborhood. The joy is in the journey.

Similarly, the observation process isn't a race to get to the application. The entire journey is filled with knowing Jesus and increasing in intimacy with Him. There is no pressure or rush. So enjoy the process. There is no urgency. Remember: the joy is in the journey.

SATURATION IN OBSERVATION

Like the kindergarten class staring intently at the goldfish, the longer the kids stared, the more they discovered. Each day as they came back and examined the fish, the more they uncovered. Do the same thing with the Word of God. That's the concept of Saturation—live in the text.

Here are five suggestions to help you better observe a passage:

1. **Reread the passage.** One of the best ways to grasp what a text says is to read it over and over. Reading a passage once is like quickly glancing at a goldfish and trying to remember what it looked like. When observing a passage, consider reading it dozens of times over several days. The more

you reread the passage (and the book it's in), the more you'll notice.

2. **Begin with the obvious.** If you've ever put a puzzle together, you know that you don't start in the middle and work outward. You begin with the edge pieces to form the frame and build inward. Similarly, begin observing the things which are plain and obvious in the text (the edge pieces) and work inward as you ask questions and look for key observations (the "what to look fors" included in Appendix 5).

3. **Keep your eyes on Christ.** Many people come to the Bible with the sole desire to find something for themselves — something that will help them feel better or a nugget they can use to prove someone wrong. It becomes selfish and inward-focused. Remember, Bible study is about knowing Jesus and being transformed by His truth. Yes, you are involved in the process, but keep your eyes on Christ and seek to know Him more.

4. **Let the text speak.** We often come to Scripture with a preconceived thought of what we want it to say rather than allowing it to speak for itself. When you observe a text, don't see it through your own "glasses" (often an individualistic, twenty-first century, Western world perspective); instead, get into the mind of the biblical author and what he is saying to his audience (more on that in step two). What does the text actually say? Don't try to make it fit what you want it to say.

5. **Slow down and saturate.** Rather than observing a text for a few minutes and putting it away the

rest of the day, consider writing your passage on a notecard and carrying the card with you. Throughout the day, pull it out, read it over, ponder the text, make observations, and ask questions. Use the back of the card to write questions and insights, which give you a starting point the next day to search for answers. And don't feel rushed; it's okay to go slow — take several days to observe and ponder a passage. Allow the text to marinate in your mind before moving on to the next step.

But before we talk about step two, we must remember that all good observations are seen within the context of the passage. We will discuss this key concept in the next chapter.

9

EVERY TEXT HAS A CONTEXT

7 types of context that give insight, depth, and meaning

*First of all, it is of the utmost [importance]
that we read through the Scriptures.
We ought not to turn over the Bible,
and pick out chapters as we please
here and there, but we should read it
carefully and regularly through.*
George Müller

In real estate, there is an adage that says three things determine the price of a house.

First, there is the location of the house. For example, a small shack on the beachfront of Florida may sell for more than a mansion in the middle of Wyoming (no offense to those who live there).

The second most important thing determining a house's price is the location. For example, a small shack on the beachfront of Florida may sell for more than a mansion in the middle of Kansas.

And they say the third most important thing which determines the price of a house is location. For example... Location. Location. Location. The three most essential things for pricing a house.

Likewise, in Bible study, three things determine the meaning of a text more than anything else: context, context, and context.

Some scholars suggest you learn more about what a passage says from the context than even the words in the passage.

WHAT IS CONTEXT?

In its simplest form, context is the words or sentences that give meaning to what is said.

We use context to determine the meaning of words in every sentence we speak or hear. For example, what do I mean if I say the word "coach"? It could refer to an athletic trainer, a horse-drawn carriage, or the seats in the back of an airplane. So how would you know which meaning I'm referring to? You'd know by the context of the sentence.

As another example, if I came up to you and said, "I'm green," what could I mean? Here are some potential options:

- My name is Mr. Green

- I'm Irish

- I'm the color green

- I'm sick

- I like to garden (a green thumb)

- I'm a newbie (greenhorn)
- I'm wealthy
- I'm environmentally concerned
- I'm jealous (green with envy)
- I'm an alien (just kidding)

The only way you'd know what I mean is by the context of the phrase "I'm green." So if I said, "I woke up this morning and didn't feel well; I'm green," you'd know I was sick (or an alien).

Biblical context includes the words, sentences, and paragraphs surrounding a passage which gives insight and illuminates its meaning. Context also consists of the environment or setting in which the passage resides (e.g., history, culture, geography, etc.).

Every word in Scripture sits within a sentence; every sentence sits within a paragraph, and every paragraph sits within an even larger section. You can continue expanding the context to include the entirety of the Bible.

Word

Sentence

Paragraph

Section (sometimes a chapter)

Larger section

Book

Corpus (the writings of an author)

Old or New Testament

The entire Bible

For example, in Ephesians 1:5, Paul uses the word "adoption." The immediate context of the word is its sentence and paragraph. Those sit within the "blessing" section of Ephesians 1:3–14. The blessing section sits within the larger section of Ephesians 1–3, which sits in the context of the book of Ephesians. Ephesians is a part of the "Pauline Corpus" (a fancy term referring to all of Paul's writings: Romans to Philemon). All of Paul's writings sit within the New Testament, and the context for the New Testament is the entire Bible.

> **He predestined us to adoption as sons through Jesus Christ to Himself, according to the kind intention of His will...**
>
> Ephesians 1:5

So if you want to know what Paul means by the word "adoption," you can look up the meaning of the word, examine its immediate context in the sentence and paragraph, and also see how Paul uses the word throughout his other writings (paying close attention to its use in the book of Ephesians). You may also want to discover how the word is used in other books of the Bible.

Don't be overwhelmed! The point is that every word and sentence sits within a greater and greater context, and it is the context that gives meaning to a passage.

A TEXT OUT OF CONTEXT

When we take a word or a concept out of its context, thus making it say whatever we want it to (rather than what it actually means), we call that "proof-texting." Proof-texting is commonly used to prove your point with a passage without paying attention to its context.

A humorous illustration is told of a man trying to discern God's will for his life. In desperation, he cried out to God, "Show me Your will!" and flipped open his Bible and pointed to a random passage, hoping God would give him direction and inspiration. He read, "Judas went out and hung himself." Concerned, he closed the Bible, let it flop open again, and randomly placed his finger upon another passage. This one read, "Go and do likewise."

Obviously, this is not the best way to seek God's will. As it has been said, "I can do all things through a Bible verse taken out of context." Or "a text without a context is a pretext for a proof-text."[12] The moment you take any verse and yank it out of its context, you set yourself up to misunderstand the passage.

Over the years, I've collected dozens of humorous (and disturbing) passages taken out of context. Here are a couple of my favorites. For a longer list, check out the bonus resources for this book at **deeperChristian.com/saturationbook**.

- A reason to brush your teeth every day: "My breath is offensive to my wife, and I am loathsome to my own brothers" (Job 19:17).

- A politically conservative perspective: "A wise man's heart directs him toward the right, but the foolish man's heart directs him toward the left" (Ecclesiastes 10:2).

- The single woman's favorite Bible verse: "If any man shall come after me, let him..." (Matthew 16:24). But then, of course, if the wrong men come: "I would not have you ignorant brethren." (Romans 1:13a, KJV)

- Gatorade in the Bible?: "…and Esau said to Jacob, 'Please let me have a swallow of that red stuff there, for I am famished'" (Genesis 25:30a).

---

7 TYPES OF CONTEXT IN THE BIBLE

When we talk about context, we typically refer to the words and sentences in and around a passage. Yet that is only one of seven types of context found in Scripture. When you examine and use the following seven types of context, your study will increase in insight, depth, and meaning. Let's look at each one.

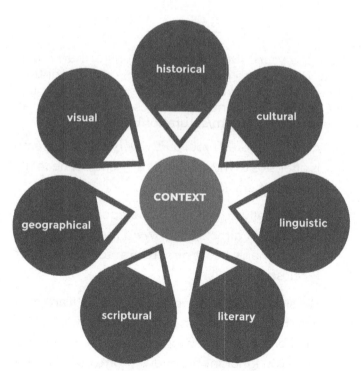

1. HISTORICAL CONTEXT

While this may sound a bit simplistic, everything in Scripture happened at some point in history — and thus must be viewed in light of what was happening historically. For example, while we use Noah and the ark as decor for our church nursery walls, the historical context of the story is found in Genesis 6, where "the LORD saw that the wickedness of man was great on the earth, and that every intent of the thoughts of his heart was only evil continually...But Noah found favor in the eyes of the LORD" (Genesis 6:5, 8). The entire flood account is about the judgment of wickedness and one family finding rescue and redemption through God's mercy and provision. Though the boat and animals are cute, I am waiting to find a mural that accurately portrays the destruction and death a worldwide flood would have caused (*though since such decor is usually on nursery walls, it may be good that we hide the death and just have smiling animals*).

The Bible often gives clues to the historical context, as in Luke 2:1 when Luke records, "Now **in those days** a decree went out from **Caesar Augustus**, that a census be taken of all the inhabited earth." Luke is highlighting something historical — that "in those days" Caesar Augustus took a census. If you don't understand the historical backdrop for those days, who Caesar Augustus was, or even what a census is, those are important facts you need to track down to understand what Luke is writing about. Those historical facts help you understand the early years of Jesus in the context of the Roman Empire.

As another example, several years before Paul wrote 1 Corinthians, there was a massive fire that destroyed much of the city. Paul uses it as an illustration in 1 Corinthians 3:12–13, which says, "Now if any man builds on the foundation with gold, silver, precious stones, wood, hay, straw, each man's work will become evident; for the day will show it because it is to be revealed with fire, and the fire itself will test the quality of each man's work." In the same way the Corinthians lost everything that was "wood, hay, and straw" yet retained that which was "gold, silver, and precious stones," Paul says so too our works will be evident in the day of judgment.

2. CULTURAL CONTEXT

Whenever people come together and do things in a certain way, they create customs and habits which become a part of their culture. Most families have a particular "culture" surrounding holidays — how you celebrate, what foods you eat, and the order of events contribute to the family culture. People groups and nations have a variety of cultures that influence mindset, preferences, food, language, beliefs, traditions, and everyday living and choices.

Culture isn't good or bad in and of itself. We must realize that everyone has cultural biases and preferences that affect thinking and decisions. And this cultural influence (context) is also found within Scripture.

For example, in Acts 1:6, the disciples ask Jesus a question that appears strange if not seen in the light of the cultural context. They ask, "Lord, is it at this time You are restoring the kingdom to Israel?" They ask a cultural question.

Rome had conquered the known world, and the Jews were praying for restoration and freedom. The cultural mindset of the Jews was that when the Messiah came, He would march down to Rome, kick Caesar off his throne, and re-establish Israel to the glory days of David and Solomon. When Jesus died, the disciples' hope of Israel's restoration died too. But when Jesus rose from the dead, they thought it was time for the conquering Messiah to defeat Rome. So they asked the question lingering in their minds: "Jesus, is now the time?!"

Jesus responded by telling them they asked the wrong question (Acts 1:7–8). Their misunderstanding came from their culture. They couldn't grasp that Jesus was doing something even more significant than a physical restoration of a temporal kingdom.

We must remember the Bible is full of context, and the cultural context changes throughout Scripture — Israel wandering in the Wilderness is a different cultural context than Israel under a King, which is different than when they are in captivity or living under Roman rule during the time of Jesus. We need to pay attention to the cultural cues in Scripture.

3. LINGUISTIC CONTEXT

This is the context we generally think of — words, their meanings, grammar, and even the original languages of Scripture (Hebrew, Greek, and some Aramaic).

GRAMMAR

Many of us have tried to forget our sixth-grade grammar lessons. But understanding the basics of grammar can help illuminate the purpose of a passage.

My favorite grammar example is the Great Commission from Matthew 28:18–20.

> And Jesus came up and spoke to them, saying, "All authority has been given to Me in heaven and on

> earth. "**Go** therefore and **make disciples** of all the nations, **baptizing** them in the name of the Father and the Son and the Holy Spirit, **teaching** them to observe all that I commanded you; and lo, I am with you always, even to the end of the age."

If you examine the grammar, you find four verbs — technically, for all the grammar nerds, there are three participles and one main verb. In short, there is one main action (verb) in the passage and three subsidiary adjectives (descriptions) that explain the main action.

Most sermons on the Great Commission focus on "going" (probably because Christians today usually don't go). Yet the Commission's command (the main verb) is not to go but to "make disciples."

We are called to make disciples, which means we must go, baptize, and teach.

Understanding the grammar helps us grasp the main focus and emphasis of Jesus' command.

TIME/TENSE

Not only is basic grammar helpful to understand, but so is the time element of a passage, also called the "tense." Is the passage describing the past, present, or future?

Romans 5:1-2 starts with a statement about our past, declares our present reality, and concludes by looking forward to our future hope.

> Therefore, having been justified by faith, we have peace with God through our Lord Jesus Christ, through whom also we have obtained our introduction by faith into this grace in which we stand; and we exult in hope of the glory of God (Romans 5:1-2).

- **Past**: having been justified by faith
- **Present**: we have peace with God through our Lord Jesus Christ
- **Present**: we exult
- **Looking to the future**: in hope of the glory of God

As you examine passages, ask yourself about the time element and "when" something happens. This is most clear in the original languages (you can use a free online tool to find the "tense" of a word), but even a good English translation will help.

WORDS AND THEIR MEANING

It's also important to know that many words have a variety of meanings (remember "coach" and "green" from earlier?). This is often called the "semantic range" of a word. Bill Mounce, a scholar who has written several books on biblical Greek, said this about translating words:

> Since a word in one language does not line up exactly with a word in another language, translation is often a matter of choosing one meaning or the other, which generally means some information is lost. It also means all translations are interpretive. Words have what is called a "semantic range," a breadth of meaning. They don't have one "literal" meaning.[13]

Mark L. Strauss, a New Testament professor, wrote about the difference between the literal and the semantic range of meaning:

> The simple answer is, words don't have literal meanings. Words have, instead, a range of potential senses. That is true of almost all words. There [are] a few words that are highly technical terms that

really only have one sense or one meaning, but almost all words in the English language have more than one meaning. They have not a literal sense, but a semantic range.

Think of the word "apple." It could be a kind of computer—a type of computer—or it could be a kind of fruit. Think of the word "cold." "Cold" could be a viral infection, as a noun, or a low temperature, as an adjective. "That is cold weather." Think of the word "table." I could say, "Set my computer on a table." Or I could say, "Let me show you this table of data." Or I could use it as a verb: "We could table this discussion." …

What determines the meaning? I'm sure you probably know the answer to that. It's the answer that we need whenever we're trying to interpret the Bible, and that is the word "context." Context determines the meaning of a word in each particular passage.[14]

This is why it is helpful to use a variety of Bible translations in your study—when you see a passage with different word choices, it signals there may be depth to a word you need to examine further. For example, Philippians 2:5 says to "have this

- mind (KJV, NKJV, ESV)

- attitude (NASB, NLT)

- mindset (NIV)

- way of thinking (LSB)

in you that was also in Christ Jesus." By reading a couple of translations, you quickly notice a range of meanings to this Greek word (*phroneō*), which should encourage you to study the word more in-depth.

As you study, examine words, their meanings, and the grammar. It may take some time but it is immensely profitable in grasping what is said. And don't be overwhelmed; there are tools that can help you (see Appendix 6).

4. LITERARY CONTEXT

Though similar to the linguistic context above, the literary context focuses on the big picture of the passage and the type of literature it is (called "genre").

We've all heard how a journalist typically asks the questions: Who? What? When? Where? Why? and How? These are also important questions in Bible study. When we step back from a passage and see the big picture of the book, it helps us understand the overarching context of who the author is, who they are writing to, and why the book was even written. We will dive into the specifics of the big picture in chapter 13.

The literary context also includes the genre of the book or passage. Though you may not use the term, you know what genre is. When you read a book or watch a movie, it sits within a particular type or category of similar writing or film.

If you see a movie poster with a man sitting on a horse wearing a cowboy hat and holding a six-shooter, you know it's a western. As a western, you expect things that are different from a sci-fi film (for example, you don't typically expect to see modern vehicles or airplanes in a western).

If a movie poster has a beautiful woman gazing lovingly at a muscular man, you know it is likely a fantasy — just kidding; it is most likely a romantic comedy or romantic drama...unless they were both wearing red and green sweaters, then you know it's one of the delightfully cheesy and predictable Hallmark Christmas movies.

If you pick up an Agatha Christie whodunit novel, you expect someone to die in an early chapter and a surprise twist at the end.

Genre gives clues for how to interpret and what is expected. The same is true for the genres within Scripture. In poetry, there is a license for imagery and metaphor. So in Psalm 91:4a, when it says God "will cover you with His pinions, and under His wings you may seek refuge…" it gives imagery for how God protects us. It is not saying God is a bird with feathers.

A parable is a story used for teaching with a primary emphasis or point. As such, not every little detail in the parable should be interpreted. In Luke 15:11–32, Jesus gives the parable of the prodigal son. The main emphasis is the response of the two sons and the father's lovingkindness. You miss the point if you try to analyze or come up with a symbolic interpretation of the famine, pigs, or what the son did in his wild living.

There are a variety of genres in Scripture, but here are the main ones you should know.[15]

- **Historical/Narrative**: the use of story and plot to explain a historical account. Though "narrative" is a term used nowadays to refer to fiction, biblical narrative is true and historical. It literally happened. (*Genesis through Ezra, Acts*)

- **Parable**: typically brief oral stories that use stereotypes, cultural concepts, and everyday activities to teach and illustrate a concept of truth. Though often simple stories, their purpose is to get people to think, reflect, evaluate, and respond. (*2 Samuel 12:1–6; Ecclesiastes 9:14–16; Matthew 13:1–53; Mark 4:1–34; Luke 15:1–16:31*)

- **Poetry**: unlike reading English poetry which often rhymes and has a certain cadence, Hebrew poetry was intended to be spoken or sung and uses vivid images, symbols, and metaphors to express truth, feelings, and experiences. Hebrew poetry is highly structured and uses parallelism (balanced lines that echo or contrast each other), word plays, chiasms, and plays on Hebrew sounds.[16] *(Job, Psalms, Proverbs, Ecclesiastes, Song of Solomon)*

- **Prophecy**: often a series of warnings intended to correct the behavior of a person or nation and often includes foretelling the future plans of God. *(Isaiah through Malachi)*

- **Biography**: typically focuses on an individual's life, sometimes contrasted with someone else. Biblical biography does not have to be chronological (though it can be). Usually, it emphasizes a selection of life events that highlight the individual's character (either positively or negatively). *(The clearest example of biography in Scripture is the Gospels — the biography of Jesus — other examples: Abraham, Isaac, Jacob, Joseph, Moses, Saul, David, Elijah)*

- **Letters/Epistles/Exposition**: a collection of exhortation, correction, and/or encouragement, typically in a well-organized logical flow. In such writing, key terms are important, and the purpose is to bring about life change and action. *(Paul's letters, Hebrews, James, 1 & 2 Peter, 1, 2, & 3 John, Jude)*

5. SCRIPTURAL CONTEXT

Some people include this concept within the linguistic or literary contexts, but what I call the Scriptural context consists of two ideas:

1. where is the location of the passage within Scripture

2. where else in the Bible does the passage (or concept) appear

The placement or order of a passage is often significant to its understanding. For example, Matthew records the Sermon on the Mount in Matthew 5–7 but then demonstrates how Jesus lived out His sermon in Matthew 8–10. Matthew specifically places chapters 8–10 to show that Jesus didn't merely preach a powerful sermon, He lived it out. Another example is in the structure of Paul's letters. He often builds an argument throughout a book, carefully placing a concept at a specific point to make an emphasis.

The other idea of the Scriptural context is if it shows up elsewhere in the Bible. The New Testament often quotes or alludes to Old Testament passages, stories, or ideas. So if you're studying the New Testament, look up the Old Testament passage, and visa versa. Additionally, if you are studying a specific word or theme, where does it first show up in Scripture, and does it give insight into the concept? Frequently, the first time a word or theme appears in Scripture, it lays the foundation for its understanding — for example, the first time "worship" shows up in the Bible is in the context of Abraham sacrificing Isaac (see Genesis 22:5), which suggests we cannot worship without sacrifice, it always costs us something to truly worship. This concept climaxes in the

New Testament when Paul says, "Therefore I urge you, brethren, by the mercies of God, to present your bodies a living and holy sacrifice, acceptable to God, which is your spiritual service of worship" (Romans 12:1). When you read a passage, consider its location based on where it shows up:

- *In the book* — what significance does this passage have in light of where it is located in the book? The author was writing with a purpose and in a specific order. How does the flow of the book impact your understanding of the passage?

- *In the writings of the same author* — does the author address the same idea elsewhere, and if so, how does that impact your understanding of the passage?

- *In all the Bible* — the Bible is ONE story made up of hundreds of smaller accounts. God has one message through His one book. How does the entire Bible inform your understanding of the passage? (Note: we will address this more in chapter 11 as we examine step three).

6. GEOGRAPHICAL CONTEXT

Everything in Scripture happened somewhere. And Scripture often presumes you know about the location and meaning of its name (just like Americans use the term "Vegas" or "Wall Street" as placeholders for concepts even beyond the location itself).

Consider using a Bible map (atlas) and discover how profitable and enriching it is to your study. Look up the location of a city, find what type of land it is

(Mediterranean coast, mountains, desert, etc.), what its climate is, and what surrounds the area. Also, consider looking up the meaning of the name (of both people and places), as there is often a play on words.

For example, the book of Ruth begins, "Now it came about in the days when the judges governed, that there was a famine in the land. And a certain man of Bethlehem in Judah went to sojourn in the land of Moab with his wife and his two sons" (Ruth 1:1).

If you look up the meaning of "Bethlehem," you discover it means "house of bread." It's ironic the house of bread had no bread in this time of famine, so Elimelech (meaning "God is my King") left with his family and sojourned in the land of Moab. Geographically, Bethlehem sits on the edge of the wilderness (a desert) about five miles south of Jerusalem, just west of the Dead Sea in the Judean mountains (about 2500 feet above sea level). They left this area to go to the land of Moab (the area of land that begins on the east side of the Dead Sea and continues up into the modern-day mountains of Jordan) — approximately fifty miles away. They didn't travel thousands of miles; it was a several-day journey by foot. Again, the locations and meaning of names become significant to the book of Ruth.

Or consider why Jesus chose Capernaum as His ministry headquarters. Capernaum (meaning "Village of Nahum" or "Village of Consolation") sits on the northern shore of the Sea of Galilee. It was a fishing village that sat at the crossroads of two major highways in Israel. Why is this significant? Because Jesus placed Himself in the middle of all trade and travel — a stop-over location for merchants and travelers going through Israel to and from Africa, Asia, or Europe. As people would come into the city of Capernaum for the night, they would look for entertainment or things to do. But the small Jewish town wouldn't have had much going on except for Jesus (who did the bulk of His teaching, ministry, and miracles there).

Again, understanding the geographical context of where things took place, what the land is like, how far distances are, and the meaning of names can enrich and deepen your study.

7. VISUAL CONTEXT

Similar to the geographical context, the visual context helps us see and experience what happened in Scripture. In the Western world, we go to a supermarket for our food, live in an air-conditioned and heated home, and travel in vehicles — all very different from the time of the Bible.

Sometimes the best way to understand a story is to put ourselves in it through the visual context. What did something look, taste, and smell like?

For example, in Mark 2, when the friends of a lame man opened a roof and lowered him to Jesus for healing, what did the houses look like (especially the roof)? In Luke 15, why does the woman have to light a lamp to search for her lost coin? In Ruth 3, what would it have looked like to watch Boaz thresh barley at the end of the harvest, and why is this visual cue important to understanding the book of Ruth? These are important visual contexts to uncover if we hope to understand those passages.

Let's examine the Luke 15 passage above in light of its visual context to see how it helps us better understand the text. Jesus tells the parable of a woman who needs to light her oil lamp to search her house for a lost coin.

Or what woman, if she has ten silver coins and loses one coin, does not light a lamp and sweep the house and search carefully until she finds it? When she has found it, she calls together her friends and neighbors, saying, "Rejoice with me, for I have found the coin which I had lost!" In the same way, I tell you, there is joy in the presence of the angels of God over one sinner who repents (Luke 15:8–10).

Houses in the times of Jesus were mainly built out of stone, with only a small opening near the top for ventilation. Windows weren't common, so the only light available in the home was from small oil lamps, which were a few inches long and could fit in the palm of your hand. These lamps often sat on shelves on the stone walls and gave off a small amount of light.[17]

Coins were small and apparently were easy to lose, as many have been found in archeological digs within the stone ruins of homes throughout Israel. With tiny coins, a small lamp, and a dark house, no wonder the woman rejoiced and celebrated when she found her lost treasure. And Jesus says this is similar to how the angels get excited over a sinner who repents.

Searching for the visual context of Scripture allows us to move beyond the text and "see" the passage afresh.

DESCRIPTIVE VS. PRESCRIPTIVE

Another critical contextual concept is determining whether a passage is descriptive or prescriptive.

Descriptive means the passage describes someone or something — it gives you the details of what happened, not telling you to do the same thing. A prescriptive passage is a clear statement that tells you to do something (like a prescription you get at the pharmacy).

The Bible contains both types of passages, and you need to know when something is a command (prescriptive) and when it merely describes something (descriptive).

For example, Jesus commands the disciples in John 15:12, "This is My commandment, that you love one another, just as I have loved you." It's rather apparent this is prescriptive; we are called to love one another. Typically, if the main verb is an imperative (command), we know it is something we are to obey. Many epistles are written this way.

Other passages are more difficult to determine. I've often heard people reference Gideon's fleece as how they determine God's will — "Then Gideon said to God, 'Do not let Your anger burn against me that I may speak once more; please let me make a test once more with the fleece, let it now be dry only on the fleece, and let there be dew on all the ground'" (Judges 6:39). They may not use a literal fleece, but their action is the same. Yet this passage *describes* what Gideon did, not what we should do in seeking God's direction.

You can obtain truth, concepts, and principles from descriptive passages (like the Old Testament histories or the Gospels and Acts from the New Testament), but you need to understand the passage in its context first and draw principles rather than specific commands from it.

Quiz yourself with the following passages. Are they descriptive or prescriptive?

1. **John 14:27** — Peace I leave with you; My peace I give to you; not as the world gives do I give to you. Do not let your heart be troubled, nor let it be fearful.

2. **Acts 2:42** — They were continually devoting themselves to the apostles' teaching and to fellowship, to the breaking of bread and to prayer.

3. **2 Kings 6:29** — So we boiled my son and ate him; and I said to her on the next day, "Give your son, that we may eat him"; but she has hidden her son.

4. **Psalm 91:2** — I will say to the LORD, "My refuge and my fortress, My God, in whom I trust!"

5. **Matthew 6:9–13** — Pray, then, in this way: "Our Father who is in heaven, Hallowed be Your name. Your kingdom come. Your will be done, on earth as it is in heaven. Give us this day our daily bread. And forgive us our debts, as we also have forgiven our debtors. And do not lead us into temptation, but deliver us from evil. For Yours is the kingdom and the power and the glory forever. Amen."

It should be evident Jesus is giving a command in #1, thus prescriptive. Though we should gather together as believers and be devoted to the teaching of the Word and prayer (a principle we can apply), #2 is descriptive because it tells us what the Early Church did, not a command they (nor us) have to follow. Hopefully, you were quick to declare #3 as descriptive rather than something we should copy. #4 and #5 are tricky because they both seem to be descriptive and prescriptive — they both describe the prayers of someone else, yet they are also the types of prayer you should pray (though you don't have to pray those words every time you approach God).

Understanding descriptive and prescriptive texts can be difficult at times, but it's important to differentiate because you don't want to take 2 Kings 6:29 as something to emulate and repeat.

QUICK SUMMARY

There is a lot in this chapter. So let me summarize everything into the following four points:

- Context is essential to understanding the meaning of a Bible passage.

- There are seven different types of biblical context to keep in mind: historical, cultural, linguistic, literary, Scriptural, geographical, and visual.

- Not all seven contexts may apply to everything you study, but think through and search out as many of the contexts as possible.

- Passages can be either descriptive (describing something) or prescriptive (a command telling us something to do).

DIVE DEEPER

In order to apply everything we've learned thus far about observations and context, I have provided a guided study that will help make this practical. Rather than skip to the next chapter, I encourage you to go through the guided observation study in Appendix 7 before we learn how to interpret the passage.

10

STEP TWO: WHAT DOES IT MEAN?

How to properly interpret a passage

*When you are reading a book
in a dark room, and come to a difficult part,
you take it to a window to get more light.
So take your Bibles to Christ.*
Robert Murray M'Cheyne

In the previous two chapters, we've examined the first step of Bible study (observation) and the importance of context. If you did the guided observation study in Appendix 7, you should have a list of observations, questions and answers, word studies, and contextual insights from Ephesians 1:4.

While you need to first observe a passage to understand what it says, it is merely bullet points and factual details unless we bring it to the second step in our process to find out what it means — interpretation. The key question is: ***What did the passage mean to the original audience?***

WHAT DO YOU THINK?

I love small group discussions, and it is a great way to share life while discussing the depth of God's Word. But there is one thing I detest about our modern small group mentality: the emphasis on personal opinion and feelings.

Too many groups gather around a circle, read a Bible passage, and ask, "so what do you think about the verse?" or "how does that make you feel?"

This will sound harsh, but I really don't care what you think or how you feel about a passage.

In Bible study, we don't voice our opinion or emotions; rather, we desire to gain God's heart, perspective, and wisdom on His Word. He declares the truth, and we must submit and say, "Yes, Lord." We will feel convicted and uncomfortable when the truth confronts our lives — but as Christians, we must not twist the meaning of a passage to fit our preference, personality, or pleasure.

As I mentioned previously, we are not to take the Word and bend it around our lives; we submit to His Word and allow God to bend (transform, change, alter) our lives around the Word. It will be uncomfortable, and we may not *feel* good about it at the time. But God is disciplining us as children so we can share in His holiness and reap a harvest of righteousness. As the writer of Hebrews reminds us,

> And have you forgotten the exhortation that addresses you as sons? "My son, do not regard lightly the discipline of the Lord, nor be weary when reproved by Him. For the Lord disciplines the one He loves, and chastises every son whom He receives." It is for discipline that you have to endure. God is treating you as sons. For what son is there whom his father does not discipline? (Hebrews 12:5-7, ESV).

Let me be blunt: God and His Word are always right, and where your life is in contradiction to Scripture, you are wrong and need His grace to change. As we interpret a passage, we must remember the interpretation is not based on our opinion, feelings, or our attempt to avoid something that confronts us. We must come humbly with a surrendered heart, the desire for God to give us insight into His Word, and a willingness for Him to radically change our lives.

THE REAL QUESTION

The central question for interpretation is not "what does it mean to me?" but rather, "what is the author saying to the original audience?" or "what did the author mean in this passage?"

This is why the first step of observation is so crucial — we must know what a passage says in context before we can determine the meaning. If we don't know what the passage says (observation), we'll never uncover what it meant to the original audience (interpretation).

We confidently believe the Holy Spirit wrote the Bible and used humans to do so (see the "Inspired" section in Appendix 2). And we believe that what is written in Scripture is not happenstance or accidental. Every word, story, and detail is important.

In determining the meaning of a passage, it's helpful to start by asking who the human author and audience was. For example, Genesis through Deuteronomy was written by Moses to the Israelites during the forty years of wilderness wandering. Matthew writes his Gospel account to the Jews, whereas Luke writes for the Gentiles. Paul writes Colossians to the church body in the city of

Colossae but writes Titus to one individual.

Discovering the author and original audience will help you correctly interpret the book's meaning. This goes back to context — knowing the author, audience, and the circumstances of why the book was written give a framework for how to understand what is said. Each human author has a different personality and background, yet the Holy Spirit used these to write His Word. The Bible is not a generic list of rules for the world; instead, God used actual people and their circumstances and personalities to declare the truth of His Word. Therefore, to know what the Bible means, we must first understand those people and circumstances.

THE GOLD NUGGET OF TRUTH

Imagine if we sat down at a coffee shop and discussed a difficult family member and how you should handle a situation that recently happened. Now imagine I gave some great advice on biblically forgiving, loving, and leading this family member to Christ. In this scenario, you would recognize that what I specifically said to you has one meaning. I am giving you wisdom for your specific situation.

After you leave the coffee shop and think back on the conversation, it would be odd to take my words and directly apply them to your finances and your question about whether to move across the country or not. That's a different context. What I said was specific to your situation with your family.

Bible study is similar. When we come to Scripture, we must figure out who the author is and what he said "in the coffeeshop" to a specific person (or group of people).

What was the original intention and meaning of the words stated?

Like a prospector who mines for gold, in the interpretation step, you look for the "gold nugget of truth" — the truth concept or the central point of the passage. What is the author saying to their original audience? What is their point?

Once you discover what the author says, I highly encourage you to reduce the statement into a single sentence you write out (sometimes called the proposition or purpose statement). Writing out the concept in a single sentence forces you to simplify the concept, helps you better understand it, and gives you a reference to look back on later.

Let's try it.

Earlier, we made some basic observations from John 15 about Jesus talking to His disciples about the vine and branches (see John 15:1–5). Review your observations (from chapter 8) and summarize what Jesus tells the disciples in a single sentence.

> It often takes extra work and a better understanding of something in order to distill it into a simple statement. We tend to ramble when the subject is complex or we don't understand it well enough.

YOUR SUMMARY SENTENCE OF JOHN 15:1–5

Here's another example for practice. Jesus says in Matthew 5:43–44, "You have heard that it was said, 'You shall love your neighbor and hate your enemy.' But I say to you, love your enemies and pray for those who persecute you..."

Though we haven't done the first step of observation, the point is rather clear. Take a moment and write a single sentence as if explaining to someone else what Jesus means in the passage as He talks to the crowd during the Sermon on the Mount.

YOUR SUMMARY SENTENCE OF MATTHEW 5:43–44

UNDERSTANDING THE PROCESS

So let's review the process so far:

1. Read and reread your passage (and the book it's in)

2. Observe and ask questions about your passage

3. Seek to understand the passage in light of its context

4. Once you have a list of observations and insights, you'll naturally begin to ask: "so what?" — "What is the author saying to his audience?"

5. Determine the meaning of the passage based on its context (i.e., what did the author mean when he spoke to his specific audience)

6. Simplify and write out the meaning (the key concept or "truth nugget") into a single sentence

THE BIBLE ONLY SAYS ONE THING

As we prayerfully interpret a passage, it is important to remember the Bible is not a trampoline that shifts and flexes its meaning based on who jumps upon it. The Bible is a rock, an unchanging foundation; thus, a text only has one meaning.

In our postmodern age, many people assume the Bible can have multiple or contradictory meanings. But again, Bible study isn't about what you think it means; we want to know what the author meant when he wrote it.

While it is true you can study a passage and come back to it later and find a greater depth, the meaning itself doesn't change; it only deepens.

As a crazy illustration (and you won't find this in Scripture), imagine a passage means, "the best kind of muffins are blueberry, and you should avoid all others." A month later, when you reread the passage, it will not change its meaning to "the best kind of muffins are chocolate, and you should avoid all others." The Bible doesn't contradict itself, and its meaning doesn't change.

Perhaps this is confusing because there are a variety of interpretations of certain passages. But I'm convinced if we all set our presuppositions aside (the assumptions we have about what Scripture says) and come honestly and humbly to the text, we'd all conclude a passage means the same thing. The problem is we often come to Scripture trying to prove a point or interpret it in light of our denominational or theological background.

As much as possible, we must be aware of our personal or theological biases and set them aside so the text can speak for itself. Theology is good, but the Bible should determine our theology, not our theology dictate our interpretation of the Bible.

A WORSHIPFUL ILLUSTRATION

For example, I grew up believing that music was at the center of worship. The pastor reinforced this idea every Sunday by saying, "Let us stand and worship," and we began to sing. No wonder I thought of music and singing whenever I read "worship" in Scripture. Yet as I studied the Bible, I found this wasn't so.

> **Abraham said to his young men, "Stay here with the donkey, and I and the lad will go over there; and we will worship and return to you."**
>
> Genesis 22:5

Again, the first time the word *worship* appears in Scripture is in the context of Abraham sacrificing Isaac on Mount Moriah (see Genesis 22:5). As you trace the concept of worship through Scripture, it is connected to sacrifice, reverence, adoration, obedience, affection, loyalty, awe, devotion, honor, service, and the manner in which we live. The word is used only occasionally in connection to praise or singing (for example, Psalm 66:4).

Ultimately, everything we do should be worship unto our King — "Whatever you do in word or deed, do all in the name of the Lord Jesus, giving thanks through Him to God the Father" (Colossians 3:17) and "Whether, then, you eat or drink or whatever you do, do all to the glory of God" (1 Corinthians 10:31).

I wasn't purposefully trying to misunderstand Scripture by thinking that worship required music and singing; I just didn't know any different.

When we come across truth, it convicts our lives and challenges how we've thought about something. In response, we will either try to force-fit the passage to make it say what we want it to (which is incredibly dangerous) or we will submit beneath the authority of God's Word and allow Him to change our heart, mind, and life.

In the interpretation step, we don't force fit Scripture to match our preferences or perspectives; we seek to understand what the author of the passage meant when he communicated with his original audience.

5 STEPS TO HELP YOU INTERPRET A PASSAGE

As you transition from making observations to interpretation, here are five steps to help you discover the meaning (the "nugget" or truth concept).

1. PRAY

Remember, you do not study independently of God but with Him. Ask Him, as the primary Author, to give you wisdom and insight into the knowledge of Himself and His Word.

2. USE YOUR OBSERVATIONS

As we come to the interpretation step, we don't ignore our observations; we use them. Look through all your observations and see what insights and common themes help you discover what the human (and divine) author is saying to his audience.

3. INTERPRET IN CONTEXT

As I've mentioned, we need to understand a verse within its context. The Bible doesn't string random thoughts together but is purposeful in everything it says. Understand the passage in the context of what the author is trying to accomplish and say in that book (i.e., the book's theme, purpose, and overall context).

Also, interpret the passage literally unless the context demands a figurative understanding. For example, the Psalms, as poetry, often include metaphors and figures of speech not meant to be literal — does God *literally* have wings (see Psalm 17:8) or is it a metaphor like the first part of the verse ("apple of the eye") for how God protects and nurtures us? Jesus isn't a literal plant (see John 15:1) or door (see John 10:7–9). So unless the passage is clearly a figure of speech or using a metaphor, interpret it literally (at face value).

A similar concept is the difference between an objective and subjective interpretation. An objective interpretation is based on the text and what it actually says (sometimes called the **inductive method**), whereas a subjective understanding is influenced by your own emotions or opinions (sometimes called the **deductive method**). When you influence the passage to say something out of context because it helps "minister to your heart" or proves a point, that is subjective (deductive) reasoning and should be avoided. While Scripture *will* minister to you and change your life, you must study objectively and allow the Word to speak for itself. Don't add extra meaning to the text.

------

4. SATURATE IN THE MEANING

Don't rush to find the interpretation. Slow down and saturate within the meaning of the passage until you truly understand it. Think through what the author is saying from a variety of angles and perspectives to make sure you have thought it through. Like a sponge in water, live in the passage and what the author says until you clearly understand and can articulate what it means.

5. WRITE A SUMMARY

One of the most helpful things I've found in the interpretation step is to write out a summary statement of the central concept or "gold nugget" in one sentence. As it has been said, "Thoughts untangle themselves through lips and pencil tips."[18] Writing out the concept helps me think through the passage more deeply and gives me a reference if I need a reminder of what the passage means. As a preacher, I also use this statement as the focus (summary) of my sermon on the passage.

Interpretation (step two) is the process of discovering the original meaning of a passage and its key concept (truth nugget) or principle. Once we know the original meaning of what the author said to his audience, we can then glean the principle from it. Just like you can take what I said at the coffeeshop about how to handle the situation with your family member and distill principles from it that you can apply to other areas of your life (like finances or whether you should move across the country), so too, you can take what the biblical author said to their original audience and understand the principle to apply it to your life.

But before we get to the application, we need to first connect it with all of Scripture. I'll show you how in the next chapter.

11

STEP THREE: HOW DOES IT CONNECT?

How to connect a passage with the whole Bible

A godly man's heart is the library to hold the Word of God; it dwells richly in him (Colossians 3:16).
Thomas Watson

When was the last time you put together a puzzle?

Whether you are a puzzle fanatic or avoider, we've all had an opportunity to hold a piece in our hands and figure out where it goes according to the picture on the box. Intuitively, you know you can't take a single puzzle piece and understand it on its own — the whole puzzle (or picture on the box) is necessary to interpret each piece.

In the Bible study process, we are now holding a piece of a puzzle. We've observed the text and discovered what the author meant. Now our passage needs to be seen in light of and connected with all of Scripture.

God has a single purpose and plan woven through the entirety of His Word — centered on and fulfilled in Jesus Christ (see Ephesians 3:11). Therefore, we must take every passage we study and see its connection to the whole of what God is saying throughout Scripture.

This was in accordance with the eternal purpose which He carried out in Christ Jesus our Lord...

Ephesians 3:11

This third step in the Bible study process is what I call "the Connection." The key question is: *How does the interpretation connect with the rest of Scripture?*

TWO REASONS TO CONNECT

When I started teaching Saturation Bible Study years ago, I only had three Bible study steps: observation, interpretation, and application. But in teaching thousands of students these concepts, I found connecting a passage with the rest of Scripture was of utmost importance for two key reasons.

1. CONNECTION GUARDS AGAINST MISINTERPRETATION

We must interpret Scripture in light of Scripture. If we take a passage and interpret it outside of its context, we will usually come to wrong and sometimes dangerous conclusions. We need to see every passage in connection to the whole counsel of God (the Bible), for it is the boundary that helps us stay faithful to Scripture.

As an example, look at 2 Kings 9:32–33:

> Then [Jehu] lifted up his face to the window and said, "Who is on my side? Who?" And two or three

officials looked down at him. He said, "Throw her [Jezebel] down." So they threw her down, and some of her blood was sprinkled on the wall and on the horses, and he trampled her under foot. Presume you conclude that, like Jehu cleansing Israel of the wickedness and impurity of Jezebel, it is okay to kill certain people if they prove themselves wicked and immoral.

Is this a reasonable interpretation? Obviously, no! Scripture tells us we are not to murder (see Exodus 20:13) and that in these days, "our struggle is not against flesh and blood, but against the rulers, against the powers, against the world forces of this darkness, against the spiritual forces of wickedness in the heavenly places" (Ephesians 6:12).

Examining 2 Kings 9:32–33 in connection with all of Scripture keeps us faithful to the text — causing us to realize we may have misunderstood the passage. Just because Jehu had Jezebel thrown down from her window does not give us the interpretive right to conclude we can do the same. It is a historical account; thus, it is descriptive, not prescriptive (see chapter 9 for a reminder). The whole of Scripture stands against murder while commanding us to love those who hate us (see Matthew 5:43–48) and to obey our governing authorities so long as they don't ask us to violate Scripture (see Romans 13).

During the connection phase, step back from your passage and test the concept (the principle; truth nugget) against all of Scripture. When an apparent contradiction presents itself, wrestle with the text and try to understand why there is tension. Work through the tension and allow it to sharpen and deepen your understanding of the passage. Often we hold fast to one passage and throw out another to confirm our theology, but remember the entire Bible contains the words of God. Rather than ignore one passage to support your conclusions, let the Word define, dictate, and direct your interpretation.[19]

2. CONNECTION GIVES EXAMPLES AND A GREATER EXPLANATION

The second benefit to connecting a passage with the rest of Scripture is that it provides examples of how the concept is lived out. Often when you study something in the New Testament, you find the concept expressed or lived out in a story of the Old Testament. Or, if you study the Old Testament, you discover the principle expressed or expanded in the New.

This helps keep the concept practical, and if you communicate, it provides biblical examples and illustrations of the concept.

For example, Leviticus 19:18 says, "You shall not take vengeance, nor bear any grudge against the sons of your people, **but you shall love your neighbor as yourself;** I am the Lord." When we connect this with all of Scripture, we find this passage often associated with the Shema (the "greatest commandment") in Deuteronomy 6:4–5. Jesus repeats it in Matthew 22:36–40 and explains it more fully in Luke 10:25–37. Look at the passages:

> **Deuteronomy 6:4–5**–Hear, O Israel! The Lord is our God, the Lord is one! You shall love the Lord your God with all your heart and with all your soul and with all your might.

> **Matthew 22:36–40**–"Teacher, which is the great commandment in the Law?" And [Jesus] said to him, "'You shall love the Lord your God with all your heart, and with all your soul, and with all your mind.' This is the great and foremost

commandment. The second is like it, 'You shall love your neighbor as yourself.' On these two commandments depend the whole Law and the Prophets."

Luke 10:25-37-And a lawyer stood up and put Him to the test, saying, "Teacher, what shall I do to inherit eternal life?" And He said to him, "What is written in the Law? How does it read to you?" And he answered, "You shall love the Lord your God with all your heart, and with all your soul, and with all your strength, and with all your mind; and your neighbor as yourself." And He said to him, "You have answered correctly; do this and you will live." But wishing to justify himself, he said to Jesus, "And who is my neighbor?" Jesus replied and said, "A man was going down from Jerusalem to Jericho, and fell among robbers, and they stripped him and beat him, and went away leaving him half dead. And by chance a priest was going down on that road, and when he saw him, he passed by on the other side. Likewise a Levite also, when he came to the place and saw him, passed by on the other side. But a Samaritan, who was on a journey, came upon him; and when he saw him, he felt compassion, and came to him and bandaged up his wounds, pouring oil and wine on them; and he put him on his own beast, and brought him to an inn and took care of him. On the next day he took out two denarii and gave them to the innkeeper and said, 'Take care of him; and whatever more you spend, when I return I will repay you.' Which of these three do you think proved to be a neighbor to the man who fell into the robbers' hands?" And he said, "The one who showed mercy toward him." Then Jesus said to him, "Go and do the same."

Our understanding of Leviticus 19:18 to "love your neighbor as yourself" is better understood and explained more fully when we connect it with other parts of Scripture.

THREE QUESTIONS TO HELP YOU SEE THE CONNECTION

To help you see your passage in light of all of Scripture, here are three starter questions to help you discover the connection:

1. Are there any verses that seem to contradict my understanding of the passage I am studying?

2. Are there any verses that can help refine my understanding of the passage I am studying? *Cross-references are sometimes helpful for this.*

3. How is this concept expressed, illustrated, or expanded in both the Old and New Testaments?

ONE BENEFIT OF READING THE BIBLE

The Connection step is one of the reasons I find tremendous benefit in reading Scripture repeatedly. The more times I read through the Bible, the more breadth of understanding I have, which helps me better connect a passage to the rest of Scripture. Again, I want to read the Bible for breadth and study it for depth.

Even if you don't have a good grasp of all of Scripture, start today and begin reading through it. Once you finish, start again. You can read the whole Bible once a year by just reading ten minutes a day. To help saturate my mind with the Word, I love listening to an audio Bible while I get ready in the morning or drive my car — you can listen to the whole Bible in about 90 hours

> **Read the Bible, read the Bible! Let no religious book take its place. Through all my perplexities and distresses, I seldom read any other book, and I as rarely felt the want of any other.**
> William Wilberforce

(or faster if you listen at 1.25 or 1.5 speed). While I may not retain everything I hear, my desire is to soak in His Word and continually fill my mind with Scripture. As I listen to the Word over and over, it is amazing how my life becomes saturated with truth and I see greater connections throughout the Word.

And while Connection is a critical step in the Bible study process, the most important one is coming up next.

12

STEP FOUR:
WHAT DOES IT CHANGE?

How to apply a passage to your life and be transformed by truth

The Scriptures were not given to increase our knowledge but to change our lives.
D.L. Moody

As I mentioned in part one, I love a good cookbook. I have dozens on my shelf, and I enjoy paging through them, looking at pictures, and imagining how scrumptious the food tastes. But what good is a cookbook if I never use it? Knowing recipes and food facts is vastly different than cooking and eating a delicious meal.

Likewise, what good is Bible study if you never apply it to your life?

Applied knowledge is often called wisdom, but knowledge without application is cerebral, useless, and often leads to pride and arrogance.

The entire Bible study process has led to this point.

If you stop before applying Scripture, you may have gained good information, but your life won't change. If you desire to grow in godliness and be "conformed to the image of Christ" (see 1 Timothy 4:7–8; 6:11; Romans 8:29), you must allow the truth of God's Word to confront and transform your heart, mind, and life.

The key application question is: **What does it change in my life?**

5 THINGS YOU NEED TO APPLY GOD'S WORD

To apply God's Word to your life, you must be intentional. Change doesn't happen by chance or coincidence. You are unlikely to become healthy and robust unless you are purposeful in your diet and exercise. Similarly, your life won't be transformed unless you purposefully allow God's Word to "pierce you." Hebrews 4:12 reminds us,

> For the word of God is living and active and sharper than any two-edged sword, and piercing as far as the division of soul and spirit, of both joints and marrow, and able to judge the thoughts and intentions of the heart.

But if you want to be pierced, judged, and changed by the Word, you must get close to it and submit yourself to its penetrating work. Here are five things you need to apply God's Word.

1. THE WORD

You won't know what to apply unless you go through the Bible study process of observation, interpretation, and connection. You need to study the text and allow God to give wisdom, understanding, truth, and the principle of the passage (the key concept or truth nugget). Once you understand the passage, the Spirit can confront (pierce and judge) your life and reveal areas that need to change. But it starts with knowing the Word.

2. HUMILITY

You must see your need revealed by God's Word and realize that you are the problem. You need the Holy Spirit to transform your life. If you approach the Word arrogantly, presuming you are right or have nothing to change, you will not listen or be open to God's work in your life. Application demands a posture of humility and surrender before the Lord in approaching His Word.

3. A PRE-DECIDED YES

When God asks us to obey, many Christians pause to consider if they want to before deciding. They want the right to say no and run the other way when conviction strikes. But what if you had a "pre-decided yes" — an attitude of "yes, Lord!" to anything He asks or reveals BEFORE He brings it up? It is a heart posture that says from the beginning, "Lord, You and Your Word are always right, and I choose to come under Your authority and truth. So before I even know what it means or how You want me to apply it practically in my life, I'm in. I say 'yes' to anything You ask or reveal." Don't reason or consider your options; choose beforehand to obey regardless of the cost.

4. OBEDIENCE

You must obey. Don't esteem obedience and then not actually obey. You have to take action. When confronted with his disobedience, King Saul told the prophet

Samuel that he kept the best of the sheep and cattle alive so he could sacrifice them to God. But Samuel replied, "Has the Lord as much delight in burnt offerings and sacrifices as in obeying the voice of the Lord? Behold, *to obey is better than sacrifice*, and to heed than the fat of rams" (1 Samuel 15:22; see also Hosea 6:6).

> **Obedience is the greatest commentary upon the Bible—Do, and thou shalt know.**
>
> Theoddore Monod

James 1:22–25 commands us,

> But prove yourselves doers of the word, and not merely hearers who delude themselves. For if anyone is a hearer of the word and not a doer, he is like a man who looks at his natural face in a mirror; for once he has looked at himself and gone away, he has immediately forgotten what kind of person he was. But one who looks intently at the perfect law, the law of liberty, and abides by it, not having become a forgetful hearer but an effectual doer, this man will be blessed in what he does.

We must not merely esteem the Words of God; we must obey and intentionally put them into action.

5. EMPOWERMENT OF THE SPIRIT

Obedience is critical for our spiritual growth, but obedience produced by our own strength, wisdom, and talent is empty (see Isaiah 64:6). We need the Spirit of God within our lives to empower and enable us to walk in obedience to His Word. So while we must obey and take action, it must be done in the strength, power, and resource of God Himself—empowered and enabled by the Holy Spirit working within us (see Ephesians 3:16, 20). For more on this, go back and review chapter 6.

YOU HAVE ALL YOU NEED

One of my favorite passages in Scripture is 2 Peter 1:2–4:

> Grace and peace be multiplied to you in the knowledge of God and of Jesus our Lord; seeing that His divine power has granted to us everything pertaining to life and godliness, through the true knowledge of Him who called us by His own glory and excellence. For by these He has granted to us His precious and magnificent promises, so that by them you may become partakers of the divine nature, having escaped the corruption that is in the world by lust.

We have everything we need for life and godliness in Christ Jesus. What do you need outside of life and godliness? Nothing.

In 2 Timothy 3:16–17, Paul reminded Timothy, "All Scripture is inspired by God and profitable for teaching, for reproof, for correction, for training in righteousness; so that the man of God may be **adequate, equipped** for every good work."

If you desire to be *adequate* (the word means "complete, qualified, capable, proficient") and *equipped* (prepared), you must allow His Word to teach, reprove, correct, and train you in righteousness. In other words, you must allow God's Word to do its sanctifying work within you.

It bears repeating, John 17:17 says, "Sanctify them in the truth; Your word is truth." The Word of God makes us holy, set apart, adequate, and equipped. God, through His indwelling Holy Spirit, desires to use His Word to confront, rebuke, pierce, conform, and transform us into holy vessels fit for His use, purpose, and glory. In short, God's Word is active in our lives to bring about godliness, holiness, and righteousness. And in Christ, we have been given everything we need for life and godliness.

DIFFERENT APPLICATION, SAME INTERPRETATION

I mentioned this before, but the Bible only says one thing. There is only one interpretation of a passage. Yes, it may have layers of depth, but the same truth.

Yet when we take the truth concept (the principle) and bring it into our lives, it will likely have a different application for each of us.

For example, let's say the concept from a passage is to love God above all things and that He desires to remove anything we've set up as an idol — something we turn to or love more than God. Bobby hears the concept and is convicted over his binge-watching of entertainment each weekend. Susie hears the same concept and is pierced about shopping. Tim wrestles over his alcohol and drug use. Jake realizes that sports have become the god he turns to. For Dan, it's video games, and Mary is confronted about the endless hours she works at her job for success and stability.

In each case, the concept from God's Word is the same, but the application is different.

As you study the Bible, God may convict you differently than others. God sanctifies and transforms us toward the same goal and standard — Jesus — but often does so in different ways, intensities, and timing. For example, there may be things God convicts and changes in your life right now that He won't deal with your best friend for another year or two.

Remain humble before God and His Word. Allow the Spirit to reveal what needs to change in your life today. And then walk in obedience, empowered by His Spirit.

QUESTIONS TO ASK

As you look at a passage you've studied and the key concept (interpretation), here are some questions to help you bring it from information to transformation.

- So what? What does it change in my life?
- What specific changes need to happen for me to live and apply this passage in my life?
- How does this concept apply personally to my life (my emotions, marriage, work, free time, family, thought life, etc.)?
- How will I obey and bring about those changes (by God's grace and enablement)?
- What is the one verse to commit to memory (that sums up the concept of the passage I studied)?
- What illustration can I create that will help remind me of the passage and the concept?
- How can I take this passage and concept and turn it into a personal prayer of surrender unto God?

Before and after you ask the questions, I encourage you to spend time in prayer and ask God:

- to reveal and teach you how you can apply the truth to your life
- to give you the grace to obey
- to plant His Word in your heart and enable it to bear fruit
- to take the information of His Word and allow it to radically transform your life

THE FRUITION OF SATURATION

The point of Saturation Bible Study is to move from having facts and information about Scripture to experiencing (ginōskō) and applying the truth in our lives.

One of the best ways to learn something is to repeat it, think about it, and rehearse it to yourself throughout the day — to meditate upon it. This is why the Psalmist said, "his delight is in the law of the LORD, and in His law he meditates day and night" (Psalm 1:2), or as Joshua 1:8 commands,

> This book of the law shall not depart from your mouth, but you shall meditate on it day and night, so that you may be careful to do according to all that is written in it; for then you will make your way prosperous, and then you will have success.

Remember, Bible study is not about an activity you check off a list; it's a lifestyle where you interact with, experience, and saturate in the Word throughout the day. Our goal is to know Christ and allow the truth of His Word to transform our lives, which means we must apply it.

THE WORST KIND OF HERESY

As we quoted earlier, James 1:22 tells us, "But prove yourselves doers of the word, and not merely hearers who delude themselves."

Jesus said the same thing when describing the difference between someone who hears His words and acts on them (likened to a man who built his house on the rock) and the person who hears His words but doesn't obey (likened to a man who built his house on sand). Jesus' emphasis is, "Why do you call Me, 'Lord, Lord,' and do not do what I say?" (Luke 6:46).

We need to not only esteem God's Word but obey it. We must move beyond accumulating head knowledge, facts, and information and allow the Word to transform our lives.

Many Christians today are concerned with biblical heresy, and rightly so. Heresy is when someone's beliefs (doctrine) is contrary to what Scripture says — and there is a lot of false and deceptive teaching that seeks to "tickle ears" and tell people what they want to hear. Paul wrote,

> "For the time will come when they will not endure sound doctrine; but wanting to have their ears tickled, they will accumulate for themselves teachers in accordance to their own desires..." (2 Timothy 4:3).

It is important for believers to stand for the truth of God's Word, be biblically accurate, and handle and speak Scripture correctly. But there is something worse than **biblical** heresy, which is **behavioral** heresy.

It breaks my heart that many people who expose false teachers in the Church are themselves arrogant, prideful, unloving, and hypocritical. They may have the correct doctrine (information), but they have not allowed the truth to affect and change their lives. They say one thing with their lips and live something different with their lives. They presume that the most important thing to have is proper head knowledge.

> **Do not expect to grow in holiness if you spend little time alone with God and do not take His Word seriously.**
>
> Joel Beeke

Head knowledge and doctrine ARE essential, but having those things is not Christianity. Christianity is not a true and false test we hope to pass — for even the demons believe and tremble (see James 2:19).

Christianity is about making Jesus Lord of our lives, being conformed to His image, and knowing Him intimately through relationship and experience (see John 17:3 and Romans 8:29).

Both our doctrine AND our behavior must align with Scripture.

This demands you intellectually know the passage you're studying *and* bring it to the point of application as you obey it.

TWO TRANSFORMATION TALES

As I've mentioned several times, learning how to saturate in God's Word has transformed my life. Let me give you two quick stories from my life.

LAYING DOWN THE LYING

I've spent a lot of time studying the book of Ephesians, going through the book verse-by-verse. The second half of chapter four is all about taking off the "former way of living" (sin) and putting on Jesus Christ. Then it gets specific; it lists things we are to take off and things we are to put on. But when I got to Ephesians 4:25, I nearly skipped it. Here's what it says:

> Therefore, putting away lying, "Let each one of you speak truth with his neighbor," for we are members of one another" (NKJV).

We are to throw off lying and put on truth.

It makes sense. I agree. But I nearly skipped it because I didn't think I had an issue with lying. I speak the truth and desire for the truth to be at the core of my life and speech.

Yet, I had not skipped studying a verse thus far, so I decided I had better study it out, thinking I might be able to use it as an exhortation for "someone else." But as I studied, I got kicked in the teeth, and began to realize that lying deals with more than just the words we speak.

> **Do not say that you believe the Bible, when you act as though it were not true.**
>
> Charles Spurgeon

I got convicted. I discovered I could speak the truth with my lips but lie with my life. For example:

- When we tell others we'll pray for them, yet never do.

- When we esteem purity and tell others that things are going well in that area, yet continue to struggle with lust.

- When we talk about the importance of being hospitable but don't do the action.

Those are lies we declare not with our lips but with our lives. But lying can also happen even while we speak true words.

My favorite example is a mother telling her son that she doesn't want him to hang out with Bertha because she is a bad influence on him. Friday night rolls around and he tells his mom that he is going to Bob's house to hang out. Several others are there when he gets to Bob's house, including Bertha. He spends a few minutes with Bob, but Bertha consumes his evening. Later, when he arrives home, his mom asks him how his time with Bob was. "Great!" he replies. True words, but he told a lie—he made his mom think he only spent time with Bob. Even if we speak true words, if what we say makes someone believe a lie, it's still called lying.

I thought Ephesians 4:25 was an easy passage that I didn't need to study because I assumed I already knew what it meant and was "good to go." Yet it became a convicting study with Jesus — He searched my heart and life, revealing areas where I spoke the truth verbally but didn't live the truth with my life. He showed me times when I allowed someone to "come to a conclusion" from what I said that wasn't accurate; I knew they misunderstood me, but since it made me look better in their eyes, I didn't want to correct it. I was confronted with the truth that I was unintentionally lying, and I had to lay the lying down at the Cross, repent, and ask for His Spirit to transform my entire life so that everything I said, did, or thought exhibited the truth.

While there are still times He convicts me of a lie I need to repent of and make right, the past several years have been incredibly freeing as I speak the truth — both with my lips and with my life.

AN EXTRAVERTED INTROVERT

One other example of how the Bible has transformed my life.

Though I deeply love people and enjoy time with others, I'm an introvert. I spend most of my days pouring into others, and I love it. But I recharge as an introvert and need time alone to pray, read, and be quiet to be refreshed.

We often think of extroverts as outgoing individuals who love people and introverts as more shy and prefer to be by themselves. But the idea is actually about how we recharge our energy. When we get tired, we tend to "default" along the spectrum of whether we want time with others or not. Extroverts often become more drained and tired at the thought of being alone because they gain energy and refreshment from being with others. In contrast, introverts tend to lean away from social situations to recharge with a small number of close family and friends or in solitude.

Not long ago, I was stirred by these words from the New Testament:

> Let brotherly love continue. Do not neglect to show hospitality to strangers...(Hebrews 13:1–2, ESV).

> Let love be without hypocrisy—by abhorring what is evil, clinging to what is good, being devoted to one another in brotherly love, giving preference to one another in honor, not lagging behind in diligence, being fervent in spirit, serving the Lord, rejoicing in hope, persevering in affliction, being devoted to prayer, contributing to the needs of the saints, pursuing hospitality (Romans 12:9–13, LSB)

I can easily justify alone time because I think I have to have it to survive. Yet, as a Christian, my life and my time are not my own; I have been bought with a price (see 1 Corinthians 6:20). According to the passages above, hospitality is evidence my love is genuine. The word "hospitable" is the Greek word *philoxenia*. While it means to show hospitality or to receive a stranger as a guest, it's a combination of the words *philos* (friend) and *xenos* (stranger). In other words, it is to befriend and be kind to a stranger. Though we have hotels for people to stay at today, in the ancient world, travelers sought the hospitality of others for accommodations and food. It was to open up your home, time, resources, and life to others.

Though I prefer to recharge in the quietness of solitude at the end of a long day, as a Christian, I'm called to show love and not neglect hospitality. Vinnie Carafano, a dear friend of mine and the leader of a ministry called King's Kids, once made a statement that deeply stirred my soul: "Extrovert may not be my nature, but it is my calling."

It is true that extroverts need time alone to seek the Lord, just as introverts need time with others. But regardless of how I prefer to recharge, my calling is to be outward-focused, show love, and practice hospitality regardless of the inconvenience and intrusion to my life. So I started to do just that. I set up the guest room in my house to always be ready to show hospitality. And unless there is a good reason why I can't, I've been saying yes to every person who has asked to stay in my home — and it's been dozens of people a year. It's pulled me out of my comfort (and preference) zone, but it's also been a lot of fun and has deepened my love for God and others.

It is one thing to study the concept of hospitality; it's another to put it into practice. If we study the Bible and don't bring it to the point of application, we may receive head knowledge, but nothing will change. We experience the transforming power of Scripture as we agree with God's Word and apply it in our lives.

> **Beware of reasoning about God's Word. Obey it.**
> Oswald Chambers

Now that we've discussed the four steps to study a passage, let's bring it together into a simple action plan.

13

THE PASSAGE PATH

The 6 stage process
to study passages

*Whenever you cannot understand a text,
open your Bible, bend your knee, and pray
over that text; and if it does not split into
atoms and open itself, try again.*
Charles Spurgeon

*A readiness to believe every promise
implicitly, to obey every command
unhesitatingly, to stand perfect and
complete in all the will of God, is the only
true spirit of Bible study.*
Andrew Murray

Following a plan speeds up the process of getting from one place to another. Just as a map does that for car trips and a workout program helps with health, we also need a plan when we study passages of Scripture.

While the specifics of your Bible study plan may morph over time (I'm continually refining mine), here are six stages you need to include on your path to study passages.

The first two are necessary before we examine specific verses, and the other four we repeat every time we come to a new verse or section.

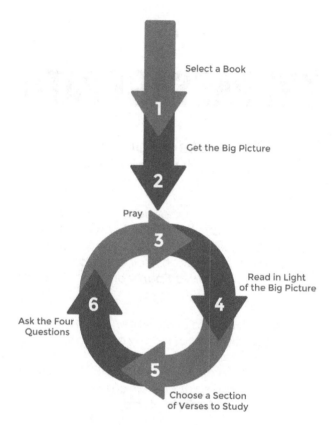

1. SELECT A BOOK

It's wildly obvious, but you need something to study.

If you are new to Bible study, I recommend starting in the New Testament, preferably with one of the shorter epistles. A short epistle can help you learn how to study without feeling daunted by dozens of chapters. Ephesians, Philippians, Colossians, 1–2 Peter, and 1 John are great books to begin with. You may also consider studying a longer passage like Luke 15, 1 Corinthians 13, etc.

As you progress in Bible study, tackle larger books in the New Testament and add some Old Testament books and passages to your queue (Ruth, Psalms, and Proverbs are great Old Testament books to start with, as well as passages such as Genesis 1–3, Exodus 3, Deuteronomy 5, Psalm 119, etc.).

Once you have a passage or book selected, it's time to gain a big-picture view.

2. GET THE BIG PICTURE

Viewing the Grand Canyon from an airplane at 30,000 feet gives you a big-picture view that is very different than hiking through the southern rim.

Similarly, at the beginning of a book or passage study, take the time to gain a 30,000-foot view. This overview is helpful to review before studying individual passages in a book to keep the overarching context in perspective. Again, context drives the meaning and our understanding of a passage (see chapter 9).

While we mentioned several of these in the chapter on context, it's helpful to review and have them forefront at the beginning of your study.

WHERE TO FIND THE INFORMATION FOR THE BIG PICTURE

There are several ways to find the needed information below. The best is to read through the book you plan to study several times and discover it yourself. It takes time but is more rewarding and helps you retain the information. Another option is to look up the information in a Bible handbook (*Talk Thru the Bible* by Wilkinson and Boa is one of my favorites).

I suggest doing the work yourself and refining it with Bible handbooks. Comparing multiple handbooks is also helpful in wrestling through various perspectives, outlines, and ideas — as certain sections (like outline and structure) may vary from guide to guide. However, if you are studying a single passage from a book and don't plan to study the entire book, it may be beneficial to start with a handbook to gain a simple overview of the book for your study.

2.1 – THE AUTHOR

Who wrote the book?

Though God is THE Author, the Spirit inspired human authors to pen the book and used their personality and vocabulary to do so. It is helpful to know details and background about the human author. For example, Matthew was an eye-witness to the life of Christ, whereas Mark wrote his Gospel from Peter's perspective. Luke was a doctor and thus added specific details none of the other Gospel writers included.

Discover as much as you can about who wrote the book.

2.2 – THE AUDIENCE

Who was the author writing to?

Each book addresses a specific group or person at a particular moment in history. What can you discover about the audience, and how does that help you understand the book?

For example, Paul wrote Colossians while a prisoner in Rome to a small church in Asia (modern-day Turkey) which was a part of the Roman Empire. But he wrote

2 Timothy to a single person not long before his execution. Also, as much as possible, keep the historical, cultural, and geographical context in mind for each audience.

Philippians has a vastly different audience and context than Leviticus. Philippians is written by Paul to a church in Macedonia — eastern Greece — under the Roman Empire. 1500 years earlier, Moses wrote Leviticus to the priests during the wilderness wandering years after the Israelites left Egypt to explain holiness and priestly duties. As you can see, the people, context, and background of these two books are vastly different.

Discover who the audience of the book is and find out as much detail as you can about them.

2.3 – THE AUTHOR'S PURPOSE OF THE BOOK
What's the point?

Every author had a purpose for writing their book. Many of Paul's letters were for correction. David wrote some Psalms to praise and magnify God and others to wrestle through life's difficulties. The prophets called the people of God to repentance. Matthew wrote to the Jews to prove that Jesus was and is the Kingly Messiah (which is why he uses so many Old Testament quotations). John tells us the purpose of his Gospel:

> "Now Jesus did many other signs in the presence of the disciples, which are not written in this book; but these are written so that you may believe that Jesus is the Christ, the Son of God, and that by believing you may have life in His name" (John 20:30–31, ESV).

The best way to discover the purpose is to read the book multiple times and discern the focus from everything the author writes. And again, Bible handbooks can be helpful.

2.4 – THE BACKGROUND

What's going on?

The more you understand the background and what happened in history, culture, and the overarching context, the better you'll understand the book.

For example, after the Israelites wandered the wilderness for forty years, they gathered together so Moses could give a final sermon — the book of Deuteronomy. Deuteronomy recounts their history and reminds them of God's laws, what God has done, and what they need to remember as they enter the Promised Land.

Fast forward 1500 years, and you find Paul writing a short letter to a man named Philemon. A slave named Onesimus stole from his master (Philemon) and ran away 1200 miles from Colossae (modern-day Turkey) to Rome. In Rome, he met Paul and became a Christian. So Paul wrote a letter to his friend Philemon and encouraged him to receive Onesimus back — not as a bond-servant (slave) but as a brother in the Lord. Rather than deal with a runaway slave as Roman law allowed, Paul urged Philemon to treat Onesimus the same way he would treat Paul if he came to visit.

Each book of the Bible has a different background and overarching context, which, when discovered, will help you better understand the depth and details of the book.

2.5 – THE GENRE

What's the category?

As previously mentioned, knowing the genre helps you interpret the book. We interpret prophecy (Jeremiah) differently than poetry (Psalms), which is different than history (Joshua). Also, remember some books contain multiple genres, like the biography of Jesus in

Matthew's Gospel which also contains parables and prophecy. For a refresher on genre, see chapter 9 under *Literary Context.*

2.6 – THE OUTLINE OF THE BOOK
What is the structure?

Scripture isn't a collection of concepts haphazardly thrown together; there is a purposeful structure and flow to what is said.

When studying a book (or large section) of the Bible, it is beneficial to create an outline. Outlining gives structure and allows you to see how each section fits together. It also helps you process each passage in light of its context and overall flow.

- To get started, read through the book multiple times, and if possible, use a printed physical copy without any chapter or verse numbers (they can often distract you from the transition points in a book...and the original text didn't include these).

For more information on how to easily create your own or buy a Bible already done for you, visit deeperChristian.com/ saturationbook

- After reading through the book (or longer passage) a couple of times, consider the significant division/ transition points of the book and give them a title (be creative and call them something memorable and helpful). For example:

Deuteronomy 1:1–4:43: What God has done (past 40 years)
Deuteronomy 4:44–26:19: What God expects (His laws)
Deuteronomy 27–34: What God will do (His covenant)

Mark 1–10: The Ministry of Jesus
Mark 11–16: The Passion of Jesus

Ephesians 1–3: Our Sitting Position (in Christ)
Ephesians 4–6: Our Walking Response

Luke 15:1-3: Why Jesus told the 3 parables
Luke 15:4-7: Parable of the Lost Sheep
Luke 15:8-10: Parable of the Lost Silver (coin)
Luke 15:11-32: Parable of the Lost Son

- Once you have the main sections, consider breaking those large sections into smaller ones. For example:

Ephesians 1–3: Our Sitting Position (in Christ)
1:1–2: Introduction and Greeting
1:3–14: Blessings in Christ
1:15–19: Paul's First Prayer
1:20–2:22: The Power of God Demonstrated
3:1–13: The Glorious Mystery
3:14–21: Paul's Second Prayer

- If you desire, and it makes sense to do so, you could break these into even smaller sub-sections.

Ephesians 1:20–2:22: The Power of God Demonstrated
1:20–23: In Christ
2:1–10: In Individuals
2:11–22: In the Church

- Once you create your outline, compare it with other outlines (in Bible handbooks or online) and test your division points against theirs. You may not agree with every outline, but tweak yours as needed. Often, seeing someone's outline helps you see things you've missed or challenges your thinking about why you divided the sections where you did).

- Keep your outline handy while doing your study so you can reference it as needed.

2.7 – THE MAJOR THEMES AND TOPICS

What's it all about?

Every book has significant themes and topics throughout it. Even short books like Amos or Philemon have at least one main topic of focus.

As you read through the book to create your outline, write down any keywords, phrases, and concepts the author repeats. For example:

- **Ephesians**: In Christ (over 30x), love (20x), grace (11x), faith (10x), body (9x), church (9x), heaven/heavenly realms (9x), walk (7x), holy/holiness (7x), mystery (6x)

- **Amos**: Lord (85x), God (33x), Israel (30x), house (25x), land (20x), citadel (12x), transgression (12x), punishment (11x), fire (9x), offering (8x)

- **Proverbs**: wise/wisdom, righteousness, wicked, way, heart, understanding, life

- **John**: Jesus, know, believe, love, life

REMINDER

Don't feel overwhelmed by the amount of detail and work in this section. Yes, it is a lot to study upfront, but the benefit to your study is incalculable. Once you work through and fill out the "Big Picture," you'll have it as an easy reference for every passage you study in that book.

Now we can dive into the study of specific verses.

To help you keep all the "Big Picture" details in one place, I've created
a worksheet for you to fill out.
You can download a PDF copy
to print and use by going to

deeperChristian.com/saturationbook

---

3. PRAY

Before engaging with the text, ask the Holy Spirit to give you insight, wisdom, and understanding into His Word.

I love using Ephesians 1:17–18 as a Bible study prayer — "God, give me a spirit of wisdom and revelation in the knowledge of You. I pray that the eyes of my heart may be enlightened..."

Take the time before every study to:

- Consecrate your heart and mind

- Surrender your life and will

- Ask for wisdom, insight, and grace to understand

- Commit to obey His Word regardless of how difficult it may be

- Declare that you desire to know Him (not just information) and that you long for the Word to sanctify and transform your life so that you might be conformed to the image of Christ

- Ask for His involvement, grace, and enablement not only in the study but to live it out

4. READ IN LIGHT OF THE BIG PICTURE

As a reminder, the concept of Saturation is to continually soak and live within Scripture like a sponge in water. One easy way to do this is to read the passage or book repeatedly. While this sounds like a large commitment, if you start with a small epistle, you should be able to read the book through in under 20 minutes.

Repetition is a great teaching tool. We don't usually remember things we've heard only once — we need repetition (which is a great teaching tool). Reading the book or section daily will help remind you of the flow and context and often gives additional insights and connections the more you read it through. If it's a long book (i.e., more than a dozen chapters), you may want to read the book once or twice a week but read the section you're studying daily. For example, if 1 John was your book, read the five chapters daily. If studying Matthew, consider reading the entire book once or twice a week but read the section you're in daily (e.g., Matthew 5–7).

If you struggle with reading the Bible or feel a bit daunted, I have several helpful hints and suggestions at deeperChristian. com/saturationbook that will help you.

When I first began studying Ephesians, I read the book daily and then also reread the section I was studying. For example, while studying Ephesians 1:3–6, I would read all of Ephesians (which takes about 25 minutes) and then reread the blessing section of Ephesians 1:3–14 (about 3 minutes). Not only did this help me connect verses in one section to other passages in the book, but it also kept the central message of Ephesians at the forefront of my mind. In other words, it allowed me to see the entire forest before I zoomed in to study one of its trees. By continually reading Ephesians, I lived in the book, metaphorically walking the streets of Ephesus daily.

If you read a book of the Bible every day for a month, even if you don't study it in-depth, you will undoubtedly see and understand more after thirty days than you did after the first day or two. Combine that with study, and you'll experience a richness of truth and understanding.

5. CHOOSE A SECTION OF VERSES TO STUDY

Now's the time to grab a verse or two and begin to soak within them. When narrowing down specific verses to study, consider if you want to do a deep dive into every verse or study by section (often paragraphs).

When I began studying Ephesians, I wanted to walk through this book verse-by-verse. When studying 2 Samuel, I took it in sections. Studying by paragraph or section allows you to go through the book faster, but a verse-by-verse study goes much deeper. And you're certainly able to do a mixture of both. One is not necessarily better than the other; it largely depends on how fast and deep you want to go.

This is where your outline (from 2.6 above) comes in handy. If you decide to study in sections, look at the first major section of your outline and start there. Let's use 1 John as an illustration. In your outline, you discover John wrote an introduction to the book in 1:1–4. So you'd start with studying these four verses as a group before moving on to the second section (1:5–10).

If you want to study each verse, it's still helpful to look at the outline to see the major sections (the immediate context). In our illustration, we'd want to start with 1 John 1:1 but see it within the specific context of 1:1–4. We'd work our way through each verse, constantly bringing it back to how it ties into the whole section.

6. ASK THE FOUR QUESTIONS

Whether you've selected a section to study or a specific verse, it's essential to ask the four questions we've examined in detail earlier in this book.

1. What does it say in context? (Observation)

2. What did it mean to the original audience? (Interpretation)

3. How does it connect with the rest of Scripture? (Connection)

4. What does it change in my life? (Application)

Remember, there is no rush in Bible study — as long as the purpose of your time is to know the Author and allow His transforming work in your life. It may take you more than a day (or even a week) to work through these four questions for the passage you are studying. That's okay. There is no rush. Take the time needed to saturate and think deeply about the verse(s). Allow the Holy Spirit to give you wisdom and insight. Ask good questions and seek out the answers. And don't forget to apply the truth in your life.

THE NERD AND HYPERACTIVE

I mentioned in chapter 7 that we are all unique. And while every plan to study Scripture should have certain elements, the actual plan may differ for each of us.

I've listed the things above we should include in our plans, but how this looks practically may be different for each of us. For example, nerds tend to love the observation step and gravitate toward going deeper and slower, doing more word studies, and geeking out over grammar and original languages. Hyperactives tend to prefer bouncing between multiple studies simultaneously. And some of us are a mixture of the two.

If you lean more nerd, don't get lost in the details and forget that Bible study is about knowing Jesus. While the details are helpful and important, we can't lose sight of our purpose to know Jesus and be transformed by truth.

If you lean more hyperactive, there is nothing wrong with doing multiple studies at a time, but don't forget to bring it to the point of application. A new study often feels more exciting than wading through endless observations, but transformation comes when we apply what we've learned. So don't rush to the new and exciting and forget to live out what you're learning.

While these six stages are a helpful guide to studying a passage, remember whichever way you lean (nerd or hyperactive), you can saturate in the passage. Take the passage with you and ponder it throughout the day. Don't let your time in the Bible be a checklist you get through so you can go live your life; allow your life to be built around and upon God's Word. Whether you want to go fast or slow, study deep or more broadly, you can apply the concept of Saturation to your study.

Also, realize different seasons of our lives may affect our study time. When creating a plan for studying Scripture, it doesn't have to be the same plan for the rest of your life. Being single, engaged, married, having a newborn, four kids under seven years old, a house full of teenagers, and retired with grandkids are all different seasons of life that may change the depth and plan of study — but in every season of life, we can still saturate and soak in Scripture so we can know Jesus more and be transformed by truth.

Even when your life gets busy, there is still time to saturate. You may not always have large chunks of dedicated time to study, but you can always take a small section of Scripture with you throughout the day to ponder, pray, and probe into its depths. Invite Jesus into your study and seek to know Him more.

LET'S DO IT TOGETHER IN THE GUIDED STUDY

One of the best ways to learn something is to actually do it. I highly encourage you to turn to Appendix 8 and join me in a guided study of Acts 1:8.

PASSAGE PATH

1. Select a Book or Passage

2. Get the Big Picture

2.1 – The Author

(Who wrote the book?)

2.2 – The Audience

(Who was the author writing to?)

2.3 – The Author's Purpose of the Book

(What's the point?)

2.4 – The Background

(What's going on?)

2.5 – The Genre

(What's the category?)

2.6 – The Outline of the Book
(What is the structure?)

2.7 – The Major Themes and Topics
(What's it all about?)

3. Pray

4. Read in Light of the Big Picture

5. Choose a Section of Verses to Study

6. Ask the FOUR QUESTIONS:

1. What does it say in context? *(Observation)*

2. What did it mean to the original audience? *(Interpretation)*

3. How does it connect with the rest of Scripture? *(Connection)*

4. What does it change in my life? *(Application)*

14

TACKLING TOPICS

9 steps to help you get the most out of a topical study

My appeal is to the Word of God. What are the reasonings, or opinions, or inferences of men? What is the chaff to the wheat? says the Lord. Let the Bible decide each question.
Horatius Bonar

My friend Eric Ludy loves to study the Bible topically. He chooses a topic and unearths what Scripture says on that theme. He has told me countless times that he thinks one of the best ways to disciple someone is to walk through key concepts of the Word and show what all of Scripture says on the topic. And it's powerful.

This systematic study helps you understand what God thinks about major topics and life issues. Do you want to know what God thinks about money, time, romance, freedom from addiction, or any other topic? Do a study on it. There is no problem in your life that isn't addressed in the Bible.

Note: though the Bible may not mention
a specific problem in your life (like an addiction
to video games), the Bible DOES address every
need and problem in our lives (it has a lot to say
about addiction, freedom, and how we spend our
time…which we can take the principles and truths
to apply to the addiction with video games).

While we have spent the majority of this book examining how to study a book or passage of the Bible (which I recommend you start with), the beauty of Saturation is that it can be done regardless of the method or focus of study. If you want to study a topic, character, or location in Scripture, you can still use what we've discussed and saturate in that topic. Let's talk about how.

TYPES OF TOPICAL STUDIES

I previously gave you the four categories I classify as topical studies. Since we study them in a similar way, I group them together:

1. **Themes** — such as sacrifice, worship, marriage, forgiveness, and prayer

2. **People** — like Abraham, Jezebel, Dorcas, and the Pharisees

3. **Places** — locations such as the desert, Dead Sea, Damascus, Dan, and Dizahab

4. **Things** — like doorways, donkeys, doves, ditches, and daggers

HOW TO STUDY A TOPIC

Here is a nine-step plan to help you tackle topics.

1. CHOOSE A TOPIC

We (obviously) need a topic to study. To get started, I suggest choosing something relevant to your life right now. Is there a question you have and need an answer to? Is there a struggle you want to overcome? Pick a topic and search out what Scripture says on the matter.

2. PRAY

Before you engage in the Word, ask the Holy Spirit to give you insight, wisdom, and understanding into His Word.

- Take the time before every study to:
- Consecrate your heart and mind
- Surrender your life and will
- Ask for wisdom, insight, and grace to understand
- Commit to obey His Word regardless of how difficult it may be
- Declare that you desire to know Him (not just information) and that you long for the Word to sanctify and transform your life so that you might be conformed to the image of Christ
- Ask for His involvement, grace, and enablement not only in the study but to live it out

3. WHAT DO YOU ALREADY KNOW? WHAT ASSUMPTIONS ARE YOU MAKING?

Before you start researching the topic, what do you already know? What assumptions do you come to the topic with?

Write down what you think the Word already says about the topic and what you presume to be correct. Be honest about your assumptions. If you desire the Word to speak and direct your thinking on the topic, you must recognize and set your assumptions aside.

For example, presume we are doing a study on the

topic of humility. I know the Bible says it's important, and I remember a verse about being clothed with humility. But I also come with the idea that humility means I need to be more quiet, unseen, and allow people to potentially take advantage of me (which, for note, is not the biblical concept of humility).

We all bring assumptions to the topic, whether those ideas are biblically accurate or not — and we need to be aware and honest of them at the start. It's helpful to take the time to think through and write down everything you know on the subject because our assumptions are often deeply ingrained, and we may not notice them at first.

After you make your list and before you dive into the Bible to see what it says on the topic, read through your list and, to the best of your ability, set these assumptions aside so God's Word can speak for itself. Also, if you've written your assumptions down, it is easier at the end of the study to compare where your understanding is correct and where it desperately needs to be changed on the topic.

4. LOOK IT UP AND WRITE IT DOWN

One of the best ways to start a topic study is to grab a concordance (or use a free online resource like blueletterbible.org) to look up words, phrases, and synonyms for your topic.

The problem with most concordances and online resources is that they are word-specific for a particular Bible translation. You will only find the specific word you search for, not variations of it. If you look for the word "love," you won't see passages that may use loving, loved, affection, intimacy, oneness, etc. As such, you will need to do various searches with similar words, phrases, and concepts. For example, to study the topic of "prayer," you would want to search words and phrases like "pray," "prayer," "ask," "supplication," "intercession," "petition," "cry out," etc.

Bonus Tip: If you use an online resource, once you find a passage with your topic included, click on the Hebrew or Greek word and look at all its uses throughout Scripture (a Hebrew or Greek word may be translated into English in various ways). For more details on how to do this, check out the bonus resources for the book at **deeperChristian.com/saturationbook**

Create a system to keep everything organized as you study. As you find passages on your topic, write them down and consider grouping them into similar sub-themes (digital copy/paste makes this easier).

Ideally, you want to examine all the passages in Scripture with the topic and similar concepts. This takes time, especially if you stay faithful to Scripture and consider the context surrounding each of the passages you look at (rather than yanking random verses out to put on your list).

5. SUMMARIZE CONCEPTS AND PRINCIPLES

Once you've explored what Scripture has to say on the topic, summarize your findings into central concepts and principles. What sub-themes does the Bible give for your topic? For example, a study on "wisdom" may have sub-themes such as "the importance of seeking wisdom," "the source of wisdom," "what is wisdom," and "the difference between wisdom and knowledge."

6. ASK QUESTIONS AND KEEP WRESTLING

Throughout the process, especially once you have summarized your study, ask questions that help you dive deeper. What passages in Scripture appear to challenge the concept or principles?

We know that Scripture does not contradict itself — so if you find a passage that seems to challenge your topic, wrestle through why it is there and how it helps you better understand your topic.

For example, we know God is love (see 1 John 4:8), and He loves the entire world (see John 3:16). But His wrath will also be revealed (see Romans 1:18, 2:5, 5:9, 12:19, etc.). These concepts seem to be opposed to one another — but since Scripture doesn't contradict itself, how do we reconcile these passages?

Processing such tensions in Scripture is helpful to fully grasp what the Bible says about your topic. Don't merely look for what you want the Bible to say; instead, ask good questions, wrestle with all of Scripture, and let the Word shape and refine what you believe about your topic.

7. CLARIFY AND SIMPLIFY

Define and summarize the topic as simply as possible in a single paragraph (preferably no more than a page).

This summary is helpful to have for future reference. I also encourage you to keep your study notes with the summary in case you want to look up specific details.

To take this a step further, consider reducing the summary paragraph into a concise sentence that gives the fundamental concept. How would you explain the topic to someone if you only had one sentence?

8. CHECK

Before you finish, consider exploring your topic in a Bible dictionary or other Bible resource to "check your work." For example, you can take a few of your key passages on the topic and read commentaries on those specific passages or look up the topic in a Bible encyclopedia that often gives articles on major topics, themes, people, and places. If your understanding of the topic differs significantly from the resource, go back and re-examine the topic. If there are slight differences, use the resource to help push back on your study and think it through on another level.

Remember, we are not trying to prove our point or preference. Instead, we desire to know what God's Word says on a topic so we can submit our understanding and lives to His truth.

9. APPLY

I've repeatedly stated that Bible study is not for information but for transformation. When you finish your study, spend time and allow the Holy Spirit to examine your life and reveal any area that needs to change. Don't merely esteem the Word, be transformed by it.

SATURATING TOPICALLY

To harken back to the concept of Saturation: regardless of how we study or whether we lean more nerd or hyperactive, we can soak, permeate, and marinate our lives in the Word of God. Don't think of a topical study as a checklist item; rather, take the topic with you throughout the day to ponder, ask questions, and think about it from various angles. Mentally walk around your topic and see what you can discover. How does your topic connect with other key themes and concepts throughout Scripture? Are there accounts in the Bible that illustrate (for good or for bad) what it means to live out your topic practically?

The point is, no matter if you want to study topics, people, themes, locations, or passages, invite the Author into the study, ponder His Word throughout the day, grow in greater intimacy with Him, and allow Him through His Word to radically transform every aspect of your life. Be a sponge that is plunged into the bucket of water called Scripture, and allow the Word to soak and saturate your life.

LET'S DO IT TOGETHER IN THE GUIDED STUDY

One of the best ways to learn something is to actually do it. I encourage you to turn to Appendix 9 and join me in a guided study on the topic of humility.

TACKLING TOPICS

1. Choose a Topic

2. Pray

3. What do you already know?
What assumptions are you making?

4. Look it up and write it down

5. Summarize concepts and principles

6. Ask questions and keep wrestling

7. Clarify and simplify

8. Check

9. Apply

15

OKAY...NOW WHAT?!

How to be a volcano of truth to your world

*We shall not adjust our Bible to the age;
but, by God's grace, we shall adjust
the age to the Bible.*
Charles Spurgeon

Now what?!

I hear the question often, and you may be asking that yourself. So, where do we go from here?

This may sound overly simplistic and perhaps childish, but I don't mean it that way. When you get done reading t rough the Bible, start over. When you finish studying a book of the Bible, pick another and jump in. When you finish studying a topic, discover what God says about another one. In other words, don't stop.

What if you had the goal to study every book of the Bible before you die? What if you wanted to grasp every major topic and theme in Scripture? While some books and topics may take more time and intensity than others, seek to know the whole Word of God and the holy God of the Word.

THE VOLCANO

While the focus of this book has been on how to study God's Word and saturate within its pages, I want to briefly mention an important dynamic that happens when we engage with the Bible.

As God gives insight into a passage and your life is transformed, you won't be able to hold it inside. Like a volcano, it will start to rumble and want to burst forth from your life. Even if your personality is quiet and shy, you will notice a desire to have an outflow for truth.

The following are some ideas on how to allow the volcanic truth that God teaches you (and uses to transform your life) to bubble forth. You won't gravitate to everything listed below, but experiment with a few and find at least one way to share what God and His Word are doing in your life.

1. JOURNAL

Journaling your reflections and insights from the Word can be simple and personal. Write the passage, what you discovered, what God taught you, and how He used it to transform your life. You may want to include a prayer of surrender, practical application points, etc. Recording your study is immensely helpful later on when you want to reference and remind yourself about what a passage means. You may think you'll never forget, but there is a reason God continually told the Israelites to remember, create stones of remembrance, to take His words and "tie them as symbols on your hands and bind them on your foreheads. Write them on the doorframes of your houses and on your gates" (Deuteronomy 6:8–9, NIV). We are prone to forget, but journaling helps us process our thoughts and becomes a way to remember.

2. FRIENDS AND FAMILY

God has placed people in your life, so share what He is teaching you (and ask them what they are learning in the Word). This is an excellent opportunity to process and verbalize truth, which deepens it in your soul. Encourage one another with the Word (see Romans 15:4, Colossians 2:2, 1 Thessalonians 5:11, and Hebrews 3:13).

3. WRITE

Consider writing a blog or article and posting it online for others to read. Whether you start an actual blog, use a social media account, or choose something similar, take what you learn and write it out so others can understand the passage and be exhorted and edified with biblical truth.

4. SPEAK

Consider starting a podcast or YouTube channel to share what you learn. Not only is this a blessing for others, but it also helps you process the truth more and deepens it in your life. As someone said, "Thoughts untangle themselves through lips and pencil tips."[20]

There are countless other options, such as teaching a small group or Sunday School class, leaving a long voicemail for a friend, etc. The point is, don't try to keep the truth in; let it bubble forth from your life like a volcanic eruption and allow God to use it to edify, equip, encourage, exhort, and admonish those around you.

16

THE ULTIMATE ADVENTURE

A revival of encountering God through His Word

Let us strive, every year we live, to become more deeply acquainted with Scripture.
J.C. Ryle

Get on your knees with an outspread Bible and linger in the presence of God.
A.W. Tozer

The American Bible Society in 2022 reported that 77% of Americans own a Bible, yet 40% of Americans never read it (an increase of 11% from 2021). Even their definition of a "Bible user" was disheartening — someone who interacts with the Bible at least three to four times *a year* outside of the church.[21]

The simple truth is that regardless of our access to Scripture, few people engage with it. We've lowered our standard so much that we consider anyone a "Bible user" who picks up a Bible more than a couple of times a year. And the time people spend reading and studying Scripture seems to decrease each year. Sadly, the Bible is becoming less important in culture, even in the church. We have more access to Scripture than ever before in human history, yet Christians know it less and less.

REVIVAL

I love the topic of revival and am deeply stirred while reading about the mighty movements of God throughout Christian history. As I've studied dozens of genuine revivals and awakenings, I've noticed that there are always three things present:

- Someone had been praying (often for years for a movement of God in their midst)
- There was a return to come under the authority of God's Word and boldly proclaim the fullness of the Gospel
- There was humility to repent from sin and turn to the centrality and sufficiency of Christ

It's not a formula we use to manipulate God into action. God WANTS to move. He longs for the nations to turn to Him. He desires "all men to be saved and to come to the knowledge of the truth" (1 Timothy 2:4). But He seeks to move amongst people who have postured themselves in humility, repentance, prayer, and beneath His Word.

Many Christians today yearn for revival (and that's good!), but are we willing to labor in prayer, turn from our wicked ways, and return to the authority of God's Word in our lives?

The only way God's Word will pierce, judge, and sanctify our lives, as Hebrews 4:12 and John 17:17 tells us, is that we must spend time in it. Just as the cleansing benefits of a bath are only available to those who sink into the waters of the tub, so too, we will never be changed or truly know our God unless we dive into the waters of the Word.

We desperately need the Word of God in our lives, marriages, families, churches, and nations.

I long for an encounter and movement of God in this generation that surpasses the Great Awakenings of old. I long for God to once again turn this world upside down (see Acts 17:6). I long for Christians to be marked by holiness and the character of God rather than by sin and the mindset of the culture. And that's been the heart behind writing this book — I want you to know God, not just know about Him. I want us to return to Scripture, intimately know the Author, and have a transformation of life (our own personal revival) — which, prayerfully, would ripple forth

> It is the students of the Bible and they alone, who will find it a weapon ready in hand in the day of battle.
>
> JC Ryle

and cause revival to ignite across our world. But if revival is ever going to take place in our generation, we need to be men and women of prayer, humility, repentance, and the Word.

THE ULTIMATE ADVENTURE

You have been given an invitation to the ultimate adventure in life. Yes, climbing Everest, bungee jumping, or kayaking down white-water rapids may thrill you, but spending time with and growing in intimacy with our God is the most exciting (and eternal) adventure we can do. I quoted Jim Elliot at the beginning of this book, but let me give you the quote again, "Oh, the fullness, pleasure, sheer excitement of knowing God on earth. I care not if I never raise my voice again for Him, if only I may love Him, please Him."[22]

God has made Himself known and longs for a relationship with you. But there is tremendous risk involved. When we see and experience God's perfection and holiness, we, like Isaiah, become freshly aware of our sin and brokenness and cry out, "Woe is me, for I am ruined! Because I am a man of unclean lips, and I live among a people of unclean lips; for my eyes have seen the King, the LORD of hosts" (Isaiah 6:5). But let us never stop pressing in and pursuing our God.

An adventure changes your life. You cannot climb Everest or jump from a plane and remain the same. It changes you. The experience forever alters your life.

This is why Saturation is the ultimate adventure. As you study God's Word to know Him and your life is transformed by His truth, you are forever altered. You cannot remain the same. In Bible study, you surrender your rights, perspective, preferences, and life unto God with the desire to be conformed to the image of Christ — no matter the risk and no matter the cost.

While I've never skydived, bungee-jumped, or climbed a mountain higher than 15000 feet, my life has been radically changed by the adventure of saturating in God's Word. And I want that same transformation in your life. *You* can know God intimately. *You* can be transformed by His Word. *You* can have revival break forth in your life. The adventure awaits.

And like any true adventure, you can read about it and put the book back on the shelf...or you can go out and live it.

So put down this book. Grab your Bible. And begin the adventure of a lifetime.

SPECIAL THANKS

First and foremost, thank You, Jesus. This has been a labor of love from You, through You, and unto You. To You alone be the glory forever and forever. Amen.

Words cannot express my deep love and appreciation for Stephen Manley, who first taught me the concept of Saturation years ago. This simple yet profound way to engage with Scripture and God Himself has forever altered my life. I am "ruined for the ordinary." Stephen, I echo Paul's words, "I thank my God upon every remembrance of you, always in every prayer of mine making request for you all with joy, for your fellowship in the gospel from the first day until now..." (Philippians 1:3-5 NKJV).

I am also eternally grateful for Eric Ludy, who gave me a greater scope and understanding of discipleship and how the individual concepts of Scripture fit into the big picture. It was also Eric who first ignited my passion for seeing Jesus in the Old Testament. I have been deeply blessed by your friendship and leadership over the years.

A special thank you to the thousands of students who have heard me teach Saturation Bible Study and allowed me to use you as guinnea pigs to test and refine the concepts with you. This book is what it is because of your patience, grace, and feedback.

I also want to thank the dozens of people who read an early manuscript and helped tighten the text. Special thanks to Ken Stewart, Kristin Martin, Danielle Beiler, and Janae Brazeal.

And for those who have helped prayerfully and financially support me and the ministry of deeperChristian over the years, I tear up thinking about how much of a blessing you have been. As Paul said, "I don't say this because I want a gift from you. Rather, I want you to receive a reward for your kindness" (Philippians 4:17 NLT). In this regard, I need to give a special thank you to Jennifer Katz, who has blessed me above and beyond for countless years.

My list could go on, for how could I not mention my parents, Dan and Sandi McConnaughey, Philip Hartman, Jalon Sommers, Zachary Phillips, Ryan Priest, Joseph Mockler, Sean and Lori Patrick, John Juneman, Jeremiah Bolich, Matt and Lizzy Zabojnik, Jessica Mullen, the Stump family, my "snuggle buddies" (A.W. Tozer, Samuel Brengle, Ian Thomas, Andrew Murray, Oswald Chambers, Leonard Ravenhill, and Corrie ten Boom), and the countless others who have blessed, encouraged, taught, and exhorted me throughout my years of Saturation.

And to you, dear reader, the mere fact you hold this book in your hands is a humble joy, blessing, and encouragement to me. I pray you've found this book helpful to press you ever deeper into Christ and His Word. Leonard Ravenhill famously said, "One of these days, some simple soul will pick up the Book of God, read it and believe it." That is my desire for you — that you not only pick up God's Word but that you read it and truly believe it, living out its grand truths and victorious reality every day for the rest of your life...and in so doing, allow God to use your life to turn the world upside down.

BONUS RESOURCES

Receive bonus resources for this book
and discover other Christ-centered
teaching by NRJohnson at

deeperChristian.com/saturationbook

APPENDIX

APPENDIX

THE STRUCTURE OF SCRIPTURE

*The Bible is shallow enough for a child
not to drown, yet deep enough for
an elephant to swim.*
Saint Augustine

One of the things I love about how God gave us His Word is that He used stories.

Though Scripture contains history, it is not a history book. It has theology but was not written as a systematic theology textbook. God did not give us a dictionary of definitions or an encyclopedia of information. He gave us stories.

Stories fascinate. They help us remember. They stir our emotions and cause us to think.

And these stories are true. The Bible is not a collection of good moral tales or legends; rather, God, in His brilliant sovereignty, utilized the literal events from history past to tell us about His nature, heart, and purpose. He reveals Himself and His redemptive plan to us through the use of story. And while the Bible is a collection of hundreds of smaller stories, there is one overarching focus, person, and purpose in view from Genesis through Revelation — Jesus Christ.

Remove Christ from the Scriptures and there is nothing left.
Martin Luther

Paul tells us that God, from eternity past, has always had a singular plan and focus. This eternal purpose has *always* been centered on Jesus Christ. Paul wrote to the Ephesians:

> To me, the very least of all saints, this grace was given, to preach to the Gentiles the unfathomable riches of Christ, and to bring to light what is the administration of the mystery which for ages has been hidden in God who created all things; so that the manifold wisdom of God might now be made known through the church to the rulers and the authorities in the heavenly places. This was in accordance with the eternal purpose which He carried out in Christ Jesus our Lord...(Ephesians 3:8–11).

Paul, addressing the Colossians, described this mystery "which has been hidden from the past ages and generations, but has now been manifested to His saints, to whom God willed to make known what is the riches of the glory of this mystery among the Gentiles, **which is Christ in you,** the hope of glory" (Colossians 1:26–27).

In his exhortation to Timothy, Paul reminds him that God,

> "who has saved us and called us with a holy calling, not according to our works, but according to **His own purpose** and grace which was **given to us in Christ Jesus from all eternity**, but now has been manifested by the appearing of our Savior Christ Jesus, who abolished death and brought life and immortality to light through the gospel" (2 Timothy 1:9–10 LSB).

Again, Paul declares that God has an eternal purpose which, from eternity past to eternity future, is given to us in Jesus. Jesus IS the plan.

Or as he told the Romans, "For from Him and through Him and to Him are all things. To Him be the glory forever" (Romans 11:36).

There has never been a plan B. The eternal purpose of our Triune God (Father, Son, and Spirit) has always been about Himself. Even before the fall of humanity in Genesis 3, Jesus was the focus — for He is "the Alpha and the Omega, the first and the last, the beginning and the end" (Revelation 22:13).

As such, the Bible is holy and wholly unique. Its aim, while giving countless substories and characters, is to focus on Jesus, the Author of the Word. The entirety of Scripture is a revelation of Jesus Christ and His redemptive work upon the Cross. Everything in Scripture points to Him. It is all about the centrality and preeminence of Christ (see Colossians 1:18).

> **The Bible is one book, written by one Author, with one subject: Jesus Christ and the salvation God...provides through Him.**
>
> Alistair Begg

In short, everything in the Old Testament leads us to Jesus Christ and the Cross, and everything in the New Testament flows from this amazing reality.

The topic of Christ being the fulfillment of all of Scripture is not the focus of this book (and perhaps another book on the theme will be forthcoming, as it is one of my favorite things to meditate upon in Scripture). But it is a foundational truth if we desire to properly understand the focus of Scripture. And with this as a backdrop, let's talk about the structure of Scripture.

THE STRUCTURE OF SCRIPTURE

Many of us take for granted the 1000+ pages clothed in leather we carry to church each Sunday. So what is this Book we call "Scripture," "God's Word," or "the Bible"?

Growing up in church, I was often told to read, study, memorize, meditate upon, and know the Bible. I spent countless hours in Sunday School with a flannel board or cut-out characters taped to toilet paper tubes to help illustrate the stories throughout Scripture. We had Bible quizzing, conferences, retreats, and weekly events all focused on this Book, yet rarely did someone stop and explain the structure of Scripture.

> **The Book of books is called the Holy Bible because it has a holy author, and aims at a holy purpose, the production of holiness in its readers.**
> Daniel Steele

So let me give you a quick overview.

The Bible is a collection of 66 books written over a span of 1400 years by approximately 40 different authors from every walk of life. And though God used various authors to write down His words, the Bible is, in fact, the very words of God (hence why we call the Bible "God's Word").

Author and scholar F.F. Bruce once described Scripture by saying:

> Any part of the human body can only be properly explained in reference to the whole body. And any part of the Bible can only be properly explained in reference to the whole Bible. The Bible, at first sight, appears to be a collection of literature–mainly Jewish. If we enquire into the circumstances under which the various Biblical documents were written, we find that they were written at intervals over a space of nearly 1400 years. The writers wrote in various lands, from Italy in the west to Mesopotamia and possibly Persia in the

east. The writers themselves were a heterogenous number of people, not only separated from each other by hundreds of years and hundreds of miles, but belonging to the most diverse walks of life. In their ranks we have kings, herdsmen, soldiers, legislators, fishermen, statesmen, courtiers, priests and prophets, a tentmaking Rabbi and a Gentile physician, not to speak of others of whom we know nothing apart from the writings they have left us. The writings themselves belong to a great variety of literary types. They include history, law (civil, criminal, ethical, ritual, sanitary), religious poetry, didactic treatises, lyric poetry, parable and allegory, biography, personal correspondence, personal memoirs and diaries, in addition to the distinctively Biblical types of prophecy and apocalyptic. For all that, the Bible is not simply an anthology; there is a unity which binds the whole together. An anthology is compiled by an anthologist, but no anthologist compiled the Bible.[23]

Don't be overwhelmed by the quote. Bruce explains that the entirety of Scripture is perfect in its unity — even though it contains a range of topics (history, law, poetry, parable, biography, personal correspondence, and prophecy, to name a few) and was written by people who were different from one another (had different jobs and education levels, lived in a variety of places, etc.). Despite the medley of its authors, no part of the Bible contradicts itself.

> There is no other book like the Bible.
> It reveals a different kind of wisdom, comes from a different source, and tells of a different love.
>
> Kevin DeYoung

The Bible isn't a collection of random ancient writings; instead, there is such perfect harmony and unity that the Bible can be explained in no other terms except that it is supernatural and God Himself wrote it. And as such, it was meant, as Jewish meditation literature,[24] to be read, re-read, and meditated upon. It was designed for us to spend our entire life saturating in and thinking upon it.

The 66 individual books that make up Scripture are grouped into two major collections: 39 books in the Old Testament (Old Covenant) and 27 books in the New Testament (New Covenant). Our modern thinking often equates "old" with irrelevant and needing to be replaced — but "old" here is best understood as the former or prior covenant. As Paul wrote Timothy, "*All* Scripture is inspired by God and profitable..." (2 Timothy 3:16). The Old is just as important and profitable as the New. Though many Christians carry around the New Testament and often ignore the Old, the Old and New Testaments are two parts of a single book with the same focus. You need both to properly understand God, His love, the Gospel, salvation, and the other major themes of Scripture.

As W.T. Purkiser wrote:

> All of the New Testament writers assumed that God's dealings with man in the history of redemption form a continuous whole, out of which whole came both the Old and New Testaments....Neither the Old Testament nor the New is fully understandable without the other. Both form two halves of a perfect-whole. The Old Testament without the New is like a head without a body. Tertullian said, "In the Old Testament the New is concealed; in the New Testament the Old is revealed."[25]

In short, what Purkiser and Tertullian are saying is that we can only properly understand the Old and New Testaments when seen in light of each other. The New is hidden all throughout the Old, and the Old is explained all throughout the New. We need both. As Christians, we are not merely New Testament believers but entire Bible believers.

These halves [Old and New Testaments] of the Bible cannot truly be separated. They deal with a single theme…throughout the whole runs an organic unity. No part could be taken out without destroying something vital to the whole. The Old Testament is incomplete without the New Testament. The New Testament requires the Old Testament as its foundation.

W.T. Purkiser

THE OLD TESTAMENT

The Old Testament contains the first 39 books of the Bible, covering approximately 4000 years of history. It begins with creation, explains the fall of humanity by sin, and describes who God is and His redemptive plan to free His people from sin. In its pages, you discover God's promises and covenants; trace the history of His chosen people through their faithfulness, desire, and obedience to God; and watch their rebellion and disobedience against Him as they seek after other gods and idols. Ultimately, you see humanity's desperate need for a Savior.

We shall not benefit from reading the Old Testament unless we look for and meditate on the glory of Christ in its pages.

John Owen

It's important to note that while the organization of the Old Testament books is not chronological, there is a purposeful arrangement to it. We divide the Old

Testament into three major sections: history, poetry (wisdom literature), and prophecy.

History
5 Books of Law (The Books of Moses: The Torah)
    Genesis
    Exodus
    Leviticus
    Numbers
    Deuteronomy
Pre-Exile History
    Joshua
    Judges
    Ruth
    1 & 2 Samuel
    1 & 2 Kings
    1 & 2 Chronicles
Post-Exile History
    Ezra
    Nehemiah
    Esther

Poetry *(which also includes the books of wisdom)*
    Job
    Psalms
    Proverbs
    Ecclesiastes
    Song of Songs (Song of Solomon)

Prophecy
Major Prophets
    Isaiah
    Jeremiah
    Lamentations
    Ezekiel
    Daniel
Minor Prophets
    Hosea
    Joel
    Amos
    Obadiah
    Jonah
    Micah
    Nahum
    Habakkuk
    Zephaniah
    Haggai
    Zechariah
    Malachi

What is the difference between the "Major Prophets" and the "Minor Prophets"?

The distinction between major and minor prophetic books is not about the importance or impact but is a literary concept determined by the length and focus of the book.

Old Testament
BOOKS IN "BIBLE ORDER"

Genesis Exodus Leviticus Numbers Deuteronomy	5 Books of Moses The Law (Torah)	History
Joshua Judges Ruth 1 Samuel 2 Samuel 1 Kings 2 Kings 1 Chronicles 2 Chronicles	Pre-Exile	
Ezra Nehemiah Esther	Post-Exile	
Job Psalms Proverbs Ecclesiastes Song of Songs	5 Books of Wisdom, Poetry, & Praise	Wisdom
Isaiah Jeremiah Lamentations Ezekiel Daniel	Major Prophets	Prophecy
Hosea Joel Amos Obadiah Jonah Micah Nahum Habakkuk Zephaniah	Pre-Exile	Minor Prophets
Haggai Zechariah Malachi	Post-Exile	

Old Testament
BOOKS IN CHRONOLOGICAL ORDER

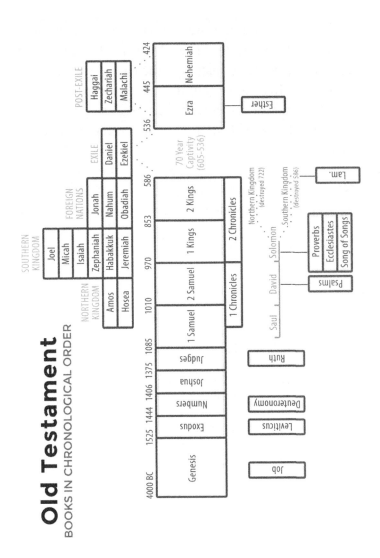

THE NEW TESTAMENT

The New Testament contains the remaining 27 books of the Bible.

The New Testament begins with the Gospels, four books containing the life and words of Jesus Christ. It continues with the history of the Early Church (Acts), includes letters of encouragement, exhortation, and warning, and concludes with the apocalyptic (prophetic/end-times) book of Revelation, which describes the return of Jesus Christ.

Again, it's important to note that the order of the New Testament books is not chronological. Still, there is a purposeful arrangement to it. It has four major sections: biography (the Gospels), history (Acts), letters (epistles) grouped by author, and apocalyptic (Revelation).

The Bible is like a telescope.
If a man looks through his telescope,
then he sees worlds beyond;
but if he looks at his telescope,
then he does not see anything but that.
The Bible is a thing to be looked through,
to see that which is beyond;
but most people only look at it;
and so they see only the dead letter.

Phillips Brooks

The Gospels *(Life and words of Jesus Christ)*
>Matthew
>Mark
>Luke
>John

History *(of the Early Church and the works of the Holy Spirit)*
>Acts

Letters *(Epistles)*
Paul's Letters to Churches *(arranged, for the most part, longest to shortest)*
>Romans
>1 & 2 Corinthians
>Galatians
>Ephesians
>Philippians
>Colossians
>1 & 2 Thessalonians

Paul's Letters to Individuals
>1 & 2 Timothy
>Titus
>Philemon

General Letters
>Hebrews
>James
>1 & 2 Peter
>1, 2, & 3 John
>Jude

Apocalyptic *(Prophecy)*
>Revelation

New Testament
BOOKS IN "BIBLE ORDER"

Matthew Mark Luke John	Gospels	Biography
Acts	Church History	History
Romans 1 Corinthians 2 Corinthians Galatians Ephesians Philippians Colossians 1 Thessalonians 2 Thessalonians	Paul's Letters to Churches	Letters
1 Timothy 2 Timothy Titus Philemon	Paul's Letters to Individuals	Letters
Hebrews James 1 Peter 2 Peter 1 John 2 John 3 John Jude	General Letters	Letters
Revelation	End Times	Prophecy

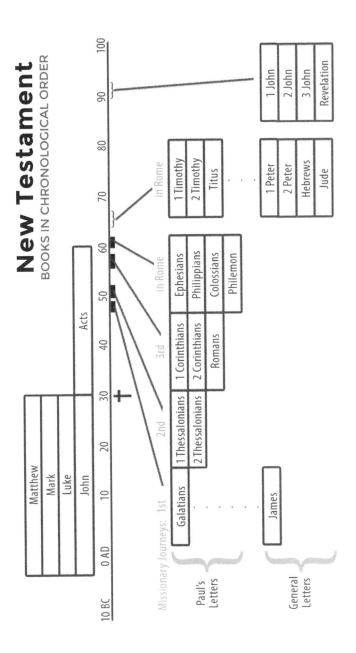

New Testament
BOOKS IN CHRONOLOGICAL ORDER

THE SUPREMACY OF SCRIPTURE

Defend the Bible?
I would just as soon defend a lion.
Just turn the Bible loose.
It will defend itself.
Charles Spurgeon

Throughout Christian history, believers knew the Bible was God's inspired Word and contained the Gospel, which, as Paul explains, "is the power of God for salvation to everyone who believes" (Romans 1:16). As such, they stood boldly for the Bible with a willingness to die for its preservation and proclamation.

As believers, we, too, must be willing to stand unashamed in our culture for the integrity of God's Word and the proclamation of the Gospel of Christ and Him crucified. But if we are going to be grounded upon the rock of Scripture, which doesn't change and is a sure foundation for every situation and season of life, we must know the nature of the Book.

Like a three-legged stool, the Bible has three aspects that describe its importance and infallibility — and all three are essential. The Bible's inspiration, inerrancy, and immutability are the reason we:

- stand immovable in our faith
- build our lives upon God's Word
- take the promises of God as a guarantee because we know they are true, and He is faithful
- have absolute confidence in the character and nature of God
- live triumphant and holy lives, unlike the world around us

INSPIRED
The authority of Scripture

When we describe Jesus (the Word of God in Person), we explain that He is 100% God and 100% man. There is a mysterious union in the incarnation — God came in the flesh. So too with Scripture (the Word of God in Text). The Bible was written 100% by men and yet 100% by God.

> **Get into the habit of saying, "Speak, Lord," and life will become a romance.**
>
> Oswald Chambers

The man Luke wrote the Gospel that bears his name; yet, while Luke put pen to paper, he was carried along by the Holy Spirit to choose specific words and record what he did. Likewise, Paul didn't write random words like we often do with a text message — even the Apostle Peter said that Paul wrote under the inspiration of God:

> "And count the patience of our Lord as salvation, just as our beloved brother Paul also wrote to

you according to the wisdom given him, as he does in all his letters when he speaks in them of these matters. There are some things in them that are hard to understand, which the ignorant and unstable twist to their own destruction, as they do the other Scriptures" (2 Peter 3:15–16, ESV).

In Christian history, this concept has often been called the inspiration of Scripture.

Paul tells Timothy that "All Scripture is *inspired by God* and profitable for teaching, for reproof, for correction, for training in righteousness..." (2 Timothy 3:16). The word "inspired" means "God-breathed" — divinely inspired, spoken by God, produced by the Spirit. And Paul clarifies it isn't "some" Scripture that is inspired, but all of it. All of Scripture are the very words of God; He is speaking to us!

> **We should read the Bible as those who listen to the very speech of God.**
> FB Meyer

The Apostle Peter emphasized the inspiration of God by writing, "But know this first of all, that no prophecy of Scripture is a matter of one's own interpretation, for no prophecy was ever made by an act of human will, but *men moved by the Holy Spirit spoke from God*" (2 Peter 1:20–21).

Scripture states that it was written under the direction and influence of God Himself. For example, in Acts 1:15–20, Peter quotes Psalm 69 and Psalm 109 and explains these psalms were written by the Holy Spirit through David to address the issue of Judas Iscariot — "Brethren, the Scripture had to be fulfilled, which the Holy Spirit foretold by the mouth of David concerning Judas..." (Acts 1:16). Or read through the first several chapters of Hebrews. Over and over, an Old

Testament passage is quoted and attributed to God ("He ever say," "He says" — e.g., Hebrews 1:5-8, 13).

The Old Testament constantly reminds us that the human authors' words weren't their own but rather "the Word of the Lord" came to them and proclaimed, "thus says the Lord."

The Bible isn't merely a good book of words written by humans — yes, it was penned by men, but the Bible contains the very words of God. He is the One speaking.

As God's Word, it must hold the authority in your life. It has the power and ability to give you orders which you must obey. You must surrender your will and preference and submit to the Word of God.

For more on the inspiration of Scripture, see Acts 1:16, 28:25, and 1 Corinthians 2:10.

INERRANT

The accuracy of Scripture

Inerrant means "without error" — God's Word is perfect and without flaw. And for note, we are not referring to a specific translation but the original writing of Scripture. Wayne Grudem explained inerrancy as believing in the "total truthfulness and reliability of God's words."[26] The Bible is true and always tells the truth.

God is perfect, holy, and without flaw. And as we already examined, the Bible is His very words. Thus the Bible is also perfect, holy, and without flaw. It is accurate.

Grab a pen and underline the statements below about how God describes His Word:

- As for God, His way is blameless; the word of the LORD is tested; He is a shield to all who take refuge in Him (2 Samuel 22:31).

- Then You came down on Mount Sinai, and spoke with them from heaven; You gave them just ordinances and true laws, good statutes and commandments (Nehemiah 9:13).

- The words of the LORD are pure words; as silver tried in a furnace on the earth, refined seven times (Psalm 12:6).

- The law of the LORD is perfect, restoring the soul; the testimony of the LORD is sure, making wise the simple. The precepts of the LORD are right, rejoicing the heart; the commandment of the LORD is pure, enlightening the eyes (Psalm 19:7–8).

- The works of His hands are truth and justice; all His precepts are sure (Psalm 111:7).

- Your word is very pure, therefore Your servant loves it (Psalm 119:140).

- Every word of God is tested; He is a shield to those who take refuge in Him (Proverbs 30:5).

- Sanctify them in the truth; Your word is truth (John 17:17).

- So then, the Law is holy, and the commandment is holy and righteous and good (Romans 7:12).

We could spend countless hours together talking about the accuracy of the Bible. Whether you want to view its accuracy from a scientific, archeological, geographic, historical, or prophetic perspective, God's Word is continually proven accurate and without error. The more we understand and uncover about science, history, geography, or _____ (name the field), the more we understand the inerrancy and infallibility of Scripture. God's Word is pure, perfect, sure, and right (see Psalm 19:7–8). It is the truth (see John 17:17), absolutely accurate, and without error.

IMMUTABLE
The unalterability of Scripture

Immutable is another big theological term meaning unchanging. God's Word doesn't shift and bend based on culture, preference, or political correctness. It is timeless, eternal, and permanent.

There has always been an attack against God's Word. "Did God really say?" has been the anthem of the enemy starting in the Garden of Eden and continuing into our present day. Society delights in sin and balks at God's perfect standard. Jesus said in John 3:19, "This is the judgment, that the Light has come into the world, and men loved the darkness rather than the Light, for their deeds were evil."

This same questioning lie, "did God really say?" is creeping into the modern Church and causing Christians to devalue the Bible and question its validity. They may still have a copy on their shelves, but many presume it's irrelevant, a collection of good stories, or needs to change because culture has changed. One example is how the Bible has been compared to a trampoline that must flex and bend with the progression of culture[27] — in short, their flawed argument is that the meaning of Scripture should change based upon what culture and society deem as good, appropriate, and right. While it may be a popular message in today's society, the mindset is dangerous and wrong.

The Bible is not flexible, nor does it bend. The Bible is an unchanging, unalterable rock, and therefore, can be the foundation of our faith. You must have something outside of yourself and your sinful preferences to be the standard by which you measure your life. Scripture is just that — an unmoving, unchanging, timeless, eternal, permanent rock. Even Jesus compared His words to a solid rock we must build our lives upon (see Matthew 7:24–27). And as you build your life and faith upon rock, it enables you to be bold, stand firm, and have unwavering confidence.

> **Fact is fact. Truth is truth. It does not matter how you feel. We do not listen to our feelings. We believe the truth of God's Word.**
> Eric Ludy

The Bible doesn't change. It is unalterable.

Another term for this is **infallible**. Infallibility declares that the Bible is authoritative and will endure forever. To be infallible is to be permanent, not able to fail or be broken. It is perfect. Jesus said in John 10:34–35 that "Scripture cannot be broken." Peter wrote, "the word of God…lives and abides forever…the word of the LORD endures forever" (1 Peter 1:23, 25, NKJV).

WHY THE BIBLE IS IMPORTANT TO YOUR LIFE

When I was a kid, I often longed for a burning bush experience or some neon sign in the sky to give me wisdom, understanding, and direction for life. I look back and laugh because I realize I wanted a clear word from the Lord about my life. Do you see the irony? I wanted God to speak to me, yet He HAS spoken! I have His words contained in The Word. The Bible is not some dull, dusty, and dry book — it is living, active, powerful, and is a double-edged sword in my life (see Hebrews 4:12).

Do you see the necessity and importance of Scripture in your life?

The Bible is alive, it speaks to me; it has feet, it runs after me; it has hands, it lays hold of me.

Martin Luther

John Wesley once said, "God Himself has condescended to teach the way. He hath written it down in a book. O give me that Book! At any price, give me the Book of God! I have it: here is knowledge enough for me. Let me be a man of one book."[28]

The Bible is God's inspired Word and is inerrant (accurate), immutable (unchanging), and infallible (perfect and permanent). He is the One speaking to you, and His Word is to have the ultimate authority in your life. He cannot lie, His promises are sure, and thus you can trust and put your confidence in what He says.

The question is not "Will God speak?" The real question is, "Will I listen, heed, and obey the Word He has spoken?"

THE BEAUTY, BLESSINGS, AND BENEFITS OF THE BIBLE

*The Bible calls itself food.
The value of food is not
in the discussion
it arouses but in the
nourishment it imparts.*
William H. Houghton

*If you want to understand Christianity,
do not shut your Bible—open it, read it!*
D. Martyn Lloyd-Jones

Scripture promises benefits and blessings to those who read and study the Bible. Though there are many more, I've condensed them into eleven categories.

1. STUDYING THE BIBLE CAUSES GROWTH AND MATURITY

You must be in the Word if you desire to grow and mature in your faith. 1 Peter 2:2–3 tells us, "like newborn babies, long for the pure milk of the word, so that by it you may grow in respect to salvation, if you have tasted the kindness of the Lord." And yet, we shouldn't be content to drink milk the rest of our lives, but rather to mature toward "steak and potatoes." As Hebrews 5:11–14 exhorts us:

> "Concerning him we have much to say, and it is hard to explain, since you have become dull of hearing. For though by this time you ought to be teachers, you have need again for someone to teach you the elementary principles of the oracles of God, and you have come to need milk and not solid food. For everyone who partakes only of milk is not accustomed to the word of righteousness, for he is an infant. But solid food is for the mature, who because of practice have their senses trained to discern good and evil."

Man of God, you cannot expect to grow in grace if you do not read the Scriptures.

Charles Spurgeon

If you are new to the faith or just learning how to study, you may need to drink a little milk, but you can't expect to fully grow and mature if you subsist on a lactose diet.

We need to be in the Word.

2. GOD'S WORD MAKES YOU SPIRITUALLY EFFECTIVE

2 Timothy 3:16–17 says, "All Scripture is inspired by God and profitable for teaching, for reproof, for correction,

for training in righteousness; so that the man of God may be adequate, equipped for every good work."

Paul says not only is Scripture divinely inspired and breathed by God, but it is also profitable in our lives. He then gives a list of how it is beneficial and useful in our lives:

- **Teaching** (doctrine): instruction on a particular subject or topic — and that instruction is always true (see John 17:17). God's Word instructs us how to think and live biblically; thus, we must align with the truth and allow the Spirit to remove any false or incorrect teaching, instruction, or doctrine within our lives.

- **Reproof**: Scripture defines the boundaries for godly living and exposes areas in our lives outside those boundaries.

- **Correction**: the Bible purifies, cleanses, and conforms us to the image of Christ. This is where the rubber meets the road and deals with the specific things in our lives that must change for us to live holy, upright, and godly lives in this present world.

- **Training in righteousness**: the instruction, training, correction, or discipline that reveals and teaches us how to live in truth and righteousness. Righteousness is the way God is and the way humanity is called to live.

In short, the Holy Spirit uses His Word to teach and train us in godly living. He uses the reproof of Scripture to bring about correction in our lives so He can, with our obedience, enable us to walk in purity, righteousness, holiness, and conformity to God's will and standard of living.

Paul clarifies the purpose for all of this: "so that the man of God may be adequate, equipped for every good work" (2 Timothy 3:17). The word "adequate" means to be complete and capable; to be furnished, equipped, or proficient with everything you need to accomplish a task or purpose. The word "equipped" is a re-emphasis of the "completeness" concept and reminds us that Scripture is not for selfish purposes but so that we become equipped and useful to God and others (also see Ephesians 2:10).

What could we do without the Book that God gave us to read? No more than any farmer who hadn't any seed!
C.T. Studd

We need to be in the Word.

3. THE BIBLE IS THE SOURCE OF TRUTH WHICH GIVES YOU GUIDANCE AND WISDOM

Truth is more than facts and details. Jesus declared that He and His Word are the truth (see John 14:6 and 17:17). As the truth, the Bible provides guidance and wisdom for daily living.

Joshua encouraged his fellow Israelites by declaring, "This Book of the Law must not depart from your mouth. Meditate on it day and night so that you may act carefully according to all that is written in it. For then you will make your way successful, and you will be wise" (Joshua 1:8).

Psalm 119:105 says: "Your word is a lamp to my feet and a light to my path."

We need to be in the Word.

4. SCRIPTURE TRAINS YOU IN RIGHTEOUSNESS AND PURITY

We live in a culture that does everything possible to get us to live like the rest of the world — but we are called to live in holiness, righteousness, and purity.

Psalm 119:9 asks the question, "How can a young man keep his way pure?" Though talking specifically about young men, the verse applies to every believer — how can you live in righteousness and purity? The

> The Bible will keep you from sin, or sin will keep you from the Bible.
>
> DL Moody

second half of the verse answers: "By keeping it according to Your word." Scripture must train your life.

Interestingly, two verses later, we are told, "Your word I have treasured *[hidden]* in my heart, that I may not sin against You" (Psalm 119:11). There is an exciting connection between keeping your way pure, living according to the Word, and hiding the Word in your heart.

We need to be in the Word.

5. THE BIBLE PRODUCES DELIGHT AND JOY WITHIN YOU

Whoever said reading or studying the Bible is boring never truly got into the Book. When you dive into God's Word, you will experience joy and delight.

Our world tries to find fulfillment in everything that can't produce it — drugs, alcohol, one-night stands, entertainment, etc. Yet Christians have access to

> I have read the Bible through a hundred times in order, and every time with increasing joy. Whenever I have started afresh it seemed like a new book to me.
>
> George Müller

the fullness of joy. Listen to what Scripture says:

- I have set the LORD continually before me; because He is at my right hand, I will not be shaken.... You will make known to me the path of life; in Your presence is fullness of joy; in Your right hand there are pleasures forever (Psalm 16:8, 11).

- [Scripture is more] desirable than gold, yes, than much fine gold; sweeter also than honey and the drippings of the honeycomb (Psalm 19:10).

- I will meditate on Your precepts, and contemplate Your ways. I will delight myself in Your statutes; I will not forget Your word (Psalm 119:15–16 NKJV).

- These things I have spoken to you so that My joy may be in you, and that your joy may be made full (John 15:11).

We need to be in the Word.

6. THE WORD OF GOD GIVES YOU ASSURANCE OF SALVATION

Are you confident that you are saved? The Word of God assures and reminds us of our amazing salvation through the work and grace of Jesus Christ.

In writing his gospel account, the apostle John reveals his purpose: "but these have been written so that you may believe that Jesus is the Christ, the Son of God; and that believing you may have life in His name" (John 20:31). Later in 1 John 5:13, he tells us, "These things I have written to you who believe in the name of the Son of

God, so that you may know that you have eternal life."

Likewise, Paul reminds us in Romans 8:15–16, "For you have not received a spirit of slavery leading to fear again, but you have received a spirit of adoption as sons by which we cry out, 'Abba! Father!' The Spirit Himself testifies with our spirit that we are children of God…"

We need to be in the Word.

7. GOD'S WORD CONVICTS, CLEANSES, AND SANCTIFIES

Sanctification is a big term we don't typically use in normal conversation. The word is used to describe the process of being freed from sin and made holy. This happens when God uses His Word to confront our lives with truth and reveals any behavior, attitude, or thought that is ungodly, doesn't belong in our lives, and needs to be repented of.

When our lives are exposed and we come to Him in humility and repentance, He washes and cleanses us with the water of His Word (see John 15:3 and Ephesians 5:25–27).

As Jesus prayed to the Father, "Sanctify them in the truth; Your word is truth" (John 17:17).

We need to be in the Word.

8. THE BIBLE GIVES YOU PEACE

You will never experience true peace outside of Jesus, for He Himself is our peace (see Ephesians 2:14 and Isaiah 9:6). In comforting His disciples, Jesus told them, "These things I have spoken to you, so that in Me you may have peace. In the world you have tribulation, but take courage; I have overcome the world" (John 16:33).

Perhaps one of the most popular books in the Bible on peace is the Psalms. Countless Christians throughout history have turned to its pages to seek comfort and peace amidst life's storms and difficulties — always finding Jesus to be the Great Shepherd who leads, comforts, and brings peace (see Psalm 23, John 10:1–18, and Hebrews 13:20).

We need to be in the Word.

9. GOD'S WORD HELPS YOU IN PRAYER

Not only does the Bible contain many prayers that are edifying to pray in your own life (see as examples: 1 Samuel 2:1–10, Psalm 3, Ephesians 3:14–21), but the Bible teaches you how to pray (see Matthew 6:9–13) and reveals the types of prayer God answers (see 1 John 5:14–16, James 5:13–16).

> **The mightier any is in the Word, the more mighty he will be in prayer.**
>
> William Gurnall

Jesus tells you, "if you abide in Me, and My words abide in you, you will ask what you desire, and it shall be done for you" (John 15:7 NKJV).

We need to be in the Word.

10. THE WORD OF GOD PRODUCES VICTORY AND SUCCESS IN YOUR LIFE

You are to live a triumphant Christian life (see Romans 8:35–39). One way to help you live victoriously is to have the Word of God within you (see number four above). Joshua 1:8 again says, "This book of the law shall not depart from your mouth, but you shall meditate on it day and night, so that you may be careful to do according to all that is written in it;

for then you will make your way prosperous, and then you will have success."

Likewise, the apostle John wrote, "I have written to you, young men, because you are strong, and the word of God abides in you, and you have overcome the evil one" (1 John 2:14b).

We need to be in the Word.

11. SCRIPTURE HELPS YOU DISCERN TRUTH AND GUARD AGAINST DECEPTION

Lies and darkness seem to increase daily in our world. There are more distractions, noise, and opinions than ever before. How can you know what is true and stand against the lies and schemes of the enemy?

Paul warned Timothy, "For the time will come when they will not endure sound doctrine; but wanting to have their ears tickled, they will accumulate for themselves teachers in accordance to their own desires, and will turn away their ears from the truth and will turn aside to myths" (2 Timothy 4:3–4). We live in such a day.

Only when you know and stand firm upon God's Word will you recognize error and lie from the truth. You must test what you hear against God's perfect and unchanging Word and be like the Bereans who "received the word with great eagerness, examining the Scriptures daily to see whether these things were so" (Acts 17:11). You must discern between good and evil and not be tossed around with every deceptive wind of teaching (see Hebrews 5:14 and Ephesians 4:14).

We need to be in the Word.

The canon-mind is the most honest, happy, holy, and healthy mind in the universe. It's a mind controlled by the person of Jesus Christ, esteeming the things that He esteems, despising the things that He despises. It is a mind in tune with Heaven, discriminating between light and darkness with the deftness of God Himself. It is a mind radically loyal to the words of Scripture, unbending in opposition, unyielding to doubt and unwavering in its allegiance.

Eric Ludy

EXCEEDINGLY GREAT AND PRECIOUS PROMISES

These are exceedingly great and precious promises from God's Word! Countless benefits are waiting for you as you read and study Scripture. Here is what King David said about the beauty and sufficiency of Scripture:

> The law of the LORD is perfect, restoring the soul; the testimony of the LORD is sure, making wise the simple. The precepts of the LORD are right, rejoicing the heart; the commandment of the LORD is pure, enlightening the eyes. The fear of the LORD is clean, enduring forever; the judgments of the LORD are true; they are righteous altogether. They are more desirable than gold, yes, than much fine gold; sweeter also than honey and the drippings of the honeycomb. Moreover, by them Your servant is warned; in keeping them there is great reward (Psalm 19:7–11).

DIVE DEEPER

Psalm 19 is a condensed version of the beauty, blessings, and benefits of the Bible found in Psalm 119. Take some time and saturate in both of these psalms and reflect upon what it says are the blessings and benefits of reading, meditating, and studying Scripture. I encourage you to read through both psalms four times. Each time reflect upon something different:

1. Read the psalm and get the overall tone and flow.

2. Read the psalm again and make a list of all the different ways (synonyms) God's Word is referred to. *Example: Law (119:1), Testimonies (119:2), Precepts (119:4), Righteous Judgments (119:7).*

3. Read the psalm again and make a list of all the things we are to do with the Word. *Example: Walk in it (119:1), Keep it (119:2), Seek Him with all our hearts (119:3).*

4. Read the psalm again and make a list of all the benefits we receive when we read and heed the Word. *Example: Our ways are established (119:5), We will have an upright heart (119:7), Our way will be pure (119:9).*

After saturating in both psalms, compare and contrast them to each other. Consider grouping your reflections into categories and/or write a summary statement.

WHAT'S YOUR PROBLEM?

True Bible-readers and Bible-searchers never find it wearisome. They like it least who know it least, and they love it most who read it most. They find it newest who have known it longest, and they find the pasture to be the richest whose souls have been the longest fed upon it. When one of our missionaries had to read a certain Book of the Old Testament through a hundred times while he was translating it, he said that he certainly enjoyed the hundredth time of reading it more than he did the first, for he understood it better, and it seemed to him to be fuller and fresher the more familiar he became with it.
Charles Spurgeon

You can always find a "good" excuse not to study the Bible. Regardless of how far-fetched those excuses might be, there are plenty of distractions and reasons we give ourselves not to spend time in the Word.

No one will ever twist your arm to read and study

God's Word. This is also true with the other essential things in life — spiritual life, physical health, quality time with family and friends, etc. We say these things are indispensable, but no deadlines or alarms alert us to their neglect. So it's easy to ignore and push them off to "another time" when it's convenient (or at least until we hit a crisis moment — for example: when we find ourselves in the hospital because we disregarded our health).

Though there are countless excuses people give for not being in the Word, I want to focus on the five most common ones. Examine your life in the Word and see if you've wrestled with any of these struggles. I hope you find that Saturation Bible Study removes every excuse and sets you free to grow in Christ through His Word.

STRUGGLE 1: TIME

Perhaps the most common excuse I've heard about spending time in God's Word is time itself — "I just don't have enough time!"

> Am I willing to trade my addiction to the world's entertainment for more time with my Bible?
>
> Leslie Ludy

We live in a busy culture, and while we have gazillions of gadgets and gizmos to help us manage and free up time, we are busier than ever. Most people today seem stressed as they rush from one activity to another. And culturally, things are only increasing in intensity, not slowing. As such, many Christians think they don't have time for the Bible.

My first job was in a Christian bookstore (remember those ancient places you had to physically visit to find a Christian book?!). When I began working there, we had a small collection of books called "devotionals" — usually a daily guide with a verse, a modern-day story, and sometimes even a short prayer, all conveniently arranged on a single page. Throughout my seven years at the bookstore, I noticed a concerning trend — our devotional section of books got more prominent, and the devotionals themselves became shorter. Our collection of devos could easily fit on a couple of shelves when I started and became multiple bookcases when I left. Devotional length went from being advertised as a "fifteen-minute devotional" to seven . . . to five . . . to three . . . eventually to a "one-minute devotional." Why? Because we just don't have enough time to spend with Jesus.

Yet I don't think time is the real issue. As an illustration, if I offered you a million dollars if you found thirty minutes a day to spend in the Word, I presume you could come up with the time. You may have to get up earlier or cut something from your life, but you'd find a way to make it happen. The issue isn't time but priority. We make time for the things that are most important to us.

But let's say hypothetically you legitimately don't have time in your day. Your schedule is packed from when you wake up to when you hit your bed for those few precious hours of rest. I still don't think time would be an excuse because Saturation solves the time dilemma. Let me explain.

Saturation is not about a certain amount of time; rather, you are to live in the Word like a fish in water. Bible reading and study isn't a "chapter a day keeps the devil away" concept. Sure, you should dedicate time each day to read the Word and study its depths, but even on days when you're extremely busy, you can ponder, memorize, think through observations, and talk to the Author about what His Word says.

We all spend large amounts of our day thinking and "wasting time" (for example, waiting in lines, at traffic lights, etc.). What if you used these spare moments to turn your attention to Scripture? What if your time in the Word wasn't about the clock because you lived in the Word?

Think of the vine and branch from John 15. Jesus declared:

> "I am the true vine, and My Father is the vinedresser. Every branch in Me that does not bear fruit, He takes away; and every branch that bears fruit, He prunes it so that it may bear more fruit. You are already clean because of the word which I have spoken to you. Abide in Me, and I in you. As the branch cannot bear fruit of itself unless it abides in the vine, so neither can you unless you abide in Me. I am the vine, you are the branches; he who abides in Me and I in him, he bears much fruit, for apart from Me you can do nothing" (15:1–5).

When does a branch abide in the vine? How much time does it abide each day? The presumption in the text is that unless the branch abides *all the time*, it will wither and die. The branch doesn't consider if it spent the appropriate amount of time abiding today; it just abides. Likewise, you should focus less on "fifteen minutes a day for Jesus" and instead live in the Word all the time.

Again, for most of us, we DO have time, and we need to use it for what is most important. But even

> Beware of saying, "I haven't time to read the Bible, or to pray"; say rather, "I haven't disciplined myself to do these things."
>
> Oswald Chambers

if you have days where there isn't much time, you can still saturate and ponder God's Word throughout your day — you can meditate on a small portion of Scripture, listen to an audio Bible, or read the Bible in the random small chunks of time we typically use to check phones or engage in social media.

And let me give you one quick word of warning about busyness. I have found Corrie ten Boom's statement incredibly true in my life: "Beware the barrenness of a busy life." When we become bullied by busyness, we often lose what is most important, especially in our spiritual lives. But as we give time and intentionality to the Bible, we become more sensitive to the Spirit and His wooing of our hearts to spend more time with Him in His Word. In short, like a good relationship, the more time we spend with someone, the more we want to — the same is certainly true with God and His Word.

Regardless of how much time you have, you can always saturate in Scripture.

STRUGGLE 2: TRAINING

A second struggle I've heard people use is that they don't know Hebrew or Greek, can't understand grammar, or never received good grades. They've never had training and thus can't study Scripture.

But their focus tends to be on gaining facts and knowledge rather than embracing the Author. When your purpose for study becomes facts and truths, you can easily miss *the* truth. Jesus said, "I am the way, and the truth, and the life; no one comes to the Father but through Me" (John 14:6). Jesus isn't a bunch of details, facts, or information to be gleaned; He is the truth itself.

When we come to the Bible, our purpose and desire must be to know the truth (Jesus), not merely gain information. Yes, information is important; facts and details matter, but your objective is to know Christ intimately — not just know about Him.

The heart of Saturation is about embracing the Author through His Word and allowing the truth to transform your life. While you will gain information and deep insight into Scripture as you study, your motive and focus is the Person of Christ. This is freeing because it means you don't have to be brilliant, good-looking, or have special training — which I'll explain more about in the next struggle.

STRUGGLE 3: TECHNIQUE

People often tell me they don't know HOW to do Bible study. They don't know the proper technique or order. The Bible gets too confusing, and they don't know what to do next. With complexity comes frustration, so they quit.

Saturation solves the struggle of technique because the pressure is more upon God than us. As I mentioned, we don't have to be clever, have special training, or know the proper technique to study God's Word. Reading Scripture is not like reading Shakespeare.

In high school, I had the "privilege" of reading a lot of Shakespeare. While I enjoyed *Romeo and Juliet* and a few of his comedies, I got lost reading the sonnets. Every couple of lines, I cried out, "huh?!" It didn't make sense. And I had another problem: Shakespeare is dead. I can't walk up to him and ask, "What does this mean?! What were you trying to say?"

Saturating in the Bible is entirely different. The Author of the Word is alive and lives within us through His indwelling Holy Spirit. Engaging with the text of Scripture is less about your brilliance, looks, training, or a special technique; it all has to do with Him. When you get to something which doesn't make sense, you have a relationship with the Author and can ask Him what it means. You likely won't hear a booming voice, but the Spirit will lead and direct you. He will use books you read, conversations you have, sermons you listen to, and He will even bring thoughts and insights into your mind. It doesn't always happen immediately, but the more you saturate and "marinate" in the Bible and the more time you give to His Word, the more you'll find the Holy Spirit guiding you into all truth.

As Jesus was in the upper room before His death and resurrection, He explained to His disciples one of the roles of the Holy Spirit.

> But I tell you the truth, it is to your advantage that I go away; for if I do not go away, the Helper will not come to you; but if I go, I will send Him to you. And He, when He comes, will convict the world concerning sin and righteousness and judgment...But when He, the Spirit of truth, comes, He will guide you into all the truth; for He will not speak on His own initiative, but whatever He hears, He will speak; and He will disclose to you what is to come. He will glorify Me, for He will take of Mine and will disclose it to you (John 16:7–8, 13–14).

Jesus said, "It is to your advantage that I go away." What?! If I were in the room, I would have interrupted and forcefully explained that it was not to our advantage for Jesus to leave. But Jesus said He would send His Spirit to us if He departed.

According to Jesus, being filled with the Holy Spirit is better than having the physical presence of Jesus with you. With further examination, it makes sense — if Jesus were physically here, He would be limited to one physical location. But when Jesus ascended into the heavenly realms and sat down at the right hand of the Father, He sent forth His Spirit to indwell each of our lives as believers. We do not have to go to a temple in Jerusalem, a throne room in Israel, or any other physical locale to talk and have a relationship with the King of kings.

Christians often desire a burning bush, to experience God like David or Daniel, or have a neon sign in the sky. They would love to have been with Jesus like His disciples, who were able to eat with Him, talk with Him, and slap Him on the back. But according to Jesus, what you and I experience now through the infilling of the Holy Spirit is better than what the disciples had before Pentecost. Yes, they got to be physically present with Jesus, but we get His Spirit living in our lives. And Scripture indicates that in eternity we get both!

In John 16, Jesus also says that the Holy Spirit will "guide you into all truth" and will "glorify Me, for He will take of Mine and will disclose it to you." The word "guide" doesn't mean to give directions but conveys the concept of grabbing your hand and taking you somewhere. So get the progression: Jesus is the truth (John 14:6), He calls His Word the truth (John 17:17), and says the Spirit of truth (i.e., the Spirit of Jesus, the Holy Spirit) will take you by the hand and lead you into all truth (i.e., Jesus and His Word).

When you have the Holy Spirit residing in and leading your life, He continually glorifies Jesus while guiding you into all truth. This radically affects your study of God's Word. The emphasis is not upon you, your ability, intellect, or training; instead, it is upon what the Spirit of God desires to reveal and say to you through His Word.

One of my friends is an older man named Joel. He spent many years homeless, living in his van. He told me he never received good grades, never finished high school, and continues to struggle with reading. Yet, he has had great insight into God's Word. Joel may not have the traditional skills, ability, talent, wisdom, or technique in Bible study, but he allows the Holy Spirit to guide him and reveal truth that transforms his life.

> **Don't settle only for spiritual food that's been "predigested" by others. Experience the joy of discovering biblical insights firsthand through your own Bible study!**
>
> Donald Whitney

Studying the Bible is far more exciting than reading Shakespeare because the Author of the Word is alive and dwells within the believer. As you read and study the Bible, spend time with the Author, ask Him what things mean, and allow the Spirit of God to bring revelation and insight to you from His Word. It may not come immediately, but as you work through the process of Saturation outlined in this book, you'll discover that Bible study has little to do with your ability, training, or technique, and instead has everything to do with Christ and His Spirit guiding you into all truth.

STRUGGLE 4: TOOLS

Many people believe Bible study is all about tools and resources. And while resources can be helpful and speed up the study process, they aren't necessary.

If you were stuck on a deserted island and all you had was a Bible, that alone would be sufficient.

Sure, tools and resources (like commentaries and dictionaries) can give additional insight and help with original languages and contextual clues. Yes, tools may be helpful, but there is no substitute for the Spirit of God.

Please note, I do think you should use resources. We live in an unprecedented age with more access to the Bible than ever before in human history. With a click of a button on your computer or phone, you can have insights into Scripture that people a generation ago spent years studying to understand.

The danger in our modern day is that too many people use tools and resources and neglect the Bible. They spend more time in the resources about the Bible than they do in the Bible.

I love using resources and tools in my study, and many are free online (see Appendix 6). But remember, tools and resources are not a replacement for the Holy Spirit in your life, and the best resource to study the Bible is the Bible itself.

STRUGGLE 5: "TO DO"

Have you ever opened the Bible only because you felt like you had to?

Bible study and reading are certainly a discipline, and sometimes you don't feel like doing it. But your time in God's Word is to be a delight, not a duty. It's a get-to, not a have-to.

Many Christians struggle with reading or studying the Bible because they don't understand the purpose of engaging the text. They see it only as a habit, a chore, or an obligation. But as we discussed in chapter 5, the purpose of Bible study is to know Jesus and be transformed by truth.

When you miss this purpose, you become engrossed in Bible information, checking it off a list, or doing it because people tell you, "that's what good Christians do." It can quickly become tedious and a "to do" you feel obligated to perform daily.

Have you ever talked with someone who's engaged to be married?

I've nearly given up on conversations with engaged couples until they've been married for a few months. During the engagement, they seem to live in la-la land. Never once have I had to go up to an engaged man and tell him to discipline himself to think about his future wife; he can't help it! He is so wrapped up in the relationship that it consumes his thinking and everyday life.

Imagine if you had that same connection with Scripture. Since the purpose of Bible study is to know the Author and your goal is to grow in intimacy, oneness, and relationship with Him, the Bible should consume your thinking and everyday life. You should desire a greater relationship with the Author and hunger to know Him more.

If you struggle to get into the Word, check your motives. Yes, there may be days you're tired or do not want to read. Still, I've found that even on those days, if I get into the Word, God draws me closer to Himself, satisfies my longing, and I leave refreshed and hungry for more of Him. If the Bible seems more like a duty and obligation, pray and ask God to turn the duty into delight and the obligation into obsession. Spend time and tell God you want to know Him, not just know about Him. Ask Him to breathe upon your time together and stir your soul towards Him.

The most foolish person in the world is the one who has the opportunity to read, absorb, digest, live in, be immersed in worship-reading the Bible, but doesn't do it because of PREOCCUPATION with other things of this world.

Rex B. Andrews

I hope you are beginning to understand that no struggle or excuse is valid when you saturate in Scripture and know the purpose of Bible study. Saturation frees us from every excuse and allows us to pursue Christ and know Him more as we soak like a sponge in His Word.

100+ QUESTIONS TO HELP YOU OBSERVE

Read the scripture, not only as history, but as a love letter from God.
Thomas Watson

For some years now, I have read through the Bible twice every year. If you picture the Bible to be a mighty tree and every word a little branch, I have shaken every one of these branches because I wanted to know what it was and what it meant.
Martin Luther

I've found that a list of questions is helpful while observing a text. While not all of these questions will pertain to every passage you study, they are a good reference tool in your "Bible study toolbox" to help you wrestle with a passage and see things you may typically overlook.

Most of these are starter questions...a good follow-up question is: "so what?" or "why?" Remember that insight often comes when you ask the question behind the question, so keep asking questions.

I've also made the list as a downloadable PDF so you can print it off and have it handy. Download your copy at **deeperChristian.com/saturationbook**.

OVERVIEW (BIG PICTURE) QUESTIONS:

- Who is the author? How does that help me understand the book/passage?

- Who is the author writing to? What can I discover about them?

- Who are the characters in the book/passage?

- What is the purpose of the book I'm studying, and how does that give insight into this particular passage?

- When and where was the book written?

- When did this book, event, or passage happen in relation to other events?

- What is the main context? *(i.e., What is happening before and after the passage?)*

- What genre is this? *(e.g., biography, prophecy, narrative, parable, poetry, proverb, exposition/epistles, etc.)*

THE CLASSIC JOURNALIST QUESTIONS:

- Who?
- What?
- When?
- Where?
- Why?
- How?

HISTORICAL BACKGROUND QUESTIONS:

- What time period in history are we dealing with?
- What is happening around the world at this time?
- What's happening at a regional or local level?
- What's happening historically at the location where this passage takes place?
- Has anything happened in the past (*especially in the Old Testament*) that gives insight into the passage?
- Is there any other historical background that would be helpful to know?

CULTURAL BACKGROUND QUESTIONS:

- Is the context of this passage Jewish, Roman, Egyptian, Babylonian, or??
- How does that context impact the passage and its implications?
- Are there any cultural clues given in the passage?

- Are there any cultural values that influence the understanding of the passage? *(e.g., honor/shame, patriarchal, communal/individual)*

- What assumptions do I have from my own cultural lens that I may be enforcing upon the passage to mean something different than the original culture?

- Is there any other cultural background information that would be helpful to know?

OLD TESTAMENT QUESTIONS:

- If studying Hebrew poetry, is parallelism being used? *(where one word or phrase is said differently, but either means the same thing or is used to establish a contrast)*

- Is there a chiasm in the text? *(where there is a parallel in phrases or thoughts leading inward to a central point)*

- How does this Old Testament passage reveal (or point to/foreshadow) Jesus Christ?

- How does the passage/concept find its fulfillment in the New Testament?

NEW TESTAMENT QUESTIONS:

- Does this New Testament passage or verse show up in Old Testament? If so, how does the original context give insight into the New Testament passage?

- Can this New Testament passage be illustrated from the Old Testament? If so, how?

PARABLE QUESTIONS:

If you are studying a parable in the New Testament, here are some questions to consider.

- What is the occasion (context) for the parable — who was the parable spoken to, why was it told, and what prompted its telling?

- Is there a clear explanation of the parable? *(Jesus often explained His parables to the disciples)*

- What is the central focus or idea of the parable? *(Note: parables have one central focus/theme)*

- What are the relevant and irrelevant details? *(Not all details matter in a parable. Because there is one central focus, you must identify what details contribute to the main theme and which ones and merely added for the sake of the story)*

- How does cultural and historical context help interpret the parable? *(A Bible dictionary or a book on Bible times and customs can be helpful as many of the parables are related to things outside our normal context — e.g., the parable of the different agriculture soils, the parable of the wise and foolish virgins, etc.)*

GEOGRAPHY QUESTIONS:

- Is there a location mentioned? If so, look it up on a Bible map.

- What kind of place is it (desert, mountain, valley, near the coast, urban, rural, etc.)?

- Has anything happened previously at this location that informs the passage I'm examining?

- Who lives in and around this location? What do we know about them?

- Who's the ruling authority at this location? *(e.g., Pharaoh, Caesar, a king, the Sanhedrin, etc.)*

- What does the name of the location mean? Does the meaning have any significance to or wordplay in the passage?

WORD QUESTIONS:

- What is the meaning of this word in its original language?

- How can I properly understand this word in light of its context?

- Do other translations use a different word or phrase? If so, why? *(e.g., Philippians 2:5 — "let this mind/ attitude/lifestyle be in you")*

- Does the original language give any pictures or illustrations that help me understand the word better? *(e.g., the Greek word baptizō–baptism–gives the picture of a cucumber being immersed in the vinegar solution and turning into a pickle)*

- How is this word used elsewhere in the book? In the writings by the same author? In the entire Bible?

SENTENCE QUESTIONS:

- Are there any words I don't know and need to look up the definitions for?

- What are the keywords in this sentence? Should I do a word study on them?

- Is there any repetition of words, phrases, or concepts? *(repetition often shows importance or emphasis — e.g., God is holy, holy, holy)*

- Is there a contrast? *(things that are different)*

- Is there a comparison? *(things that are alike)*

- Is there a list given?

- Is there a cause and effect? *(Note: sometimes the effect is given before the cause)*

- Is there a conjunction? *(e.g., and, but, for, therefore, since, because...)*

- What is the main verb?

- Who is the subject of the sentence?

- If there are pronouns, who do they refer to? *(e.g., he, she, them, they, you, me, etc.)*

- Is there any indication of time? *(i.e., when something happened)*

- Are there any figures of speech or idioms?

  » Simile: comparing two different things with a connecting word (often with *"like, as, such as"* or with the phrase *"as...so"* — e.g., *Psalm 42:1*)

  » Metaphor: an implied comparison *(e.g., John 15:5)*

  » Exaggeration (hyperbole): a purposeful exaggeration to emphasize something *(e.g., Matthew 23:24)*

» Metonymy: using the name of one object or concept to refer to another *(e.g., Mark 1:5 — "country" refers to the people not the location)*

» Synecdoche: where the whole refers to the parts or the parts refer to the whole *(e.g., "the law" in the Old Testament can refer to the Ten Commandments, the Pentateuch [the first five books, the books of Moses], or the entire Old Testament)*

» Personification: an object is given the characteristics or attributes of a person *(e.g., Isaiah 55:12)*

» Irony: saying something opposite of what you mean *(e.g., 1 Corinthians 4:8)*

» Idioms: an expression that means something different than the individual words mean in the expression *(English examples: it's raining cats and dogs, he's in a jam, underdog... Bible examples: lamp unto my feet, harden your hearts, white-washed tombs, a double-edged sword...)*

PARAGRAPH QUESTIONS:

• What are the keywords in this paragraph? Should I do a word study on them?

• Is there any repetition of words, phrases, or concepts? *(repetition often shows importance or emphasis — e.g., "In Christ" shows up 30 times throughout Ephesians 1–3)*

- Is something stated generally or specifically? *(e.g., general: "I like desserts"... specific: "I like chocolate cake")*

- Are there questions asked... or answers given? *(Note: sometimes you have a question without an answer, an answer with a presumed question, or both a question and its answer)*

- Is there dialogue? If so, who is speaking? Who are they speaking to?

- Is there a purpose statement given? *(e.g., John 20:31)*

- Is there a summary statement of a passage *(e.g., "so that" or "for this reason")*

- What is the means by which something is accomplished? *(e.g., "in the power of the Spirit")*

- Are there actions or roles of God or other people mentioned?

- Are there any emotional terms?

- What is the tone of the passage? *(e.g., affectionate, chiding, disciplinary, instructive, reproving, correcting)*

- Is there a sequence of events? *(this happened, then this happened)*

- Are there any symbols in the passage? *(a picture that represents something else — e.g., John 10:7)*

GRAMMAR QUESTIONS:

- What can the grammar of the passage tell us? *(i.e., examine each word and its contribution to the whole — nouns, verbs, adjectives, adverbs, direct objects, etc.)*

- Should I diagram this passage? *(remember 6th-grade sentence diagraming? Sometimes this can reveal how a passage breaks into its pieces)*

OTHER GREAT QUESTIONS AND THINGS TO LOOK FOR:

- Is the passage prescriptive or descriptive? *(i.e., prescriptive: tells you what to do, a command | descriptive: tells what someone else did, narrative, story)*

- Is there a logical order or progression in the passage?

- What do we learn about God's character and nature?

- What do we learn about people? *(e.g., character, nature, attitude, behavior, etc.)*

- What do we learn about how to relate with God and/or others?

- How would you describe the before and after of an event or encounter?

- How long did something take?

- Look for keywords

- Look for commands

- Look for warnings

- Look for comparisons *(things that are alike)*

- Look for contrasts *(things that are different)*

- Look for illustrations

- Look for causes and effects and reasons for doing things

- Look for promises and their conditions for fulfillment
- Look for progression from the general to the specific
- Look for progression from the specific to the general
- Look for steps of progression in a narrative or biography
- Look for results
- Look for advice, admonitions, and attitudes
- Look for connectives, articles, and prepositions
- Look for explanations
- Look for Old Testament quotes in the New Testament
- Look for paradoxes
- Look for emphasis through the use of space (*proportion*)
- Look for planned exaggerations or hyperboles
- Look for the use of the current events of the times
- Look for the force of the verbs
- Look for anything unusual or unexpected
- Look for anything that is emphasized
- Look for things that are related
- Look for things that are alike or unlike each other
- Look for things true to life

BIBLE STUDY RESOURCES TO HELP YOU OBSERVE

Visit many good books, but live in the Bible.
Charles Spurgeon

*A Bible that's falling apart
usually belongs to someone who isn't.*
Charles Spurgeon

You don't need resources to study the Bible.

I know that's a funny way to start the appendix on Bible study resources, but before we talk about specifics, you really need to know that. You **don't** need to go out and spend money to study the Bible — you just need the Bible. Many people think Bible study is all about resources (see "struggle 4" in Appendix 4), and while I agree that resources are an incredible value and help, they do not replace Scripture itself.

I love using tools and resources to help me speed up and deepen my personal study of God's Word. But they aren't required. Yet, I'm still going to suggest you use them. Confused?

Let me explain. We live in an unprecedented time in history where we have more access to Scripture than ever before. Most of us walk around with dozens of Bible translations on our smartphones, have access to countless free tools online, and can access original language details with the push of a button. So while using resources are not necessary and the *Bible* should always be our primary resource to study the Bible, it would be foolish not to leverage the tools available to us.

Many of the resources are free online (my favorite is blueletterbible.org). And while I will mention a variety of tools and resources you could spend thousands of dollars buying, my suggestion is to start with the free stuff and build your library as you go, if it's needed.

I want to start with the five most important tools to use in Bible study. I will also talk about various other helpful resources, as well as give my favorite suggestion for Bible software (both free and paid).

THE FIVE MOST IMPORTANT TOOLS

Out of all the resources you can use, the five I recommend you start with are a Bible, a Bible dictionary, a concordance, cross-references, and an atlas.

While I will give examples of resources in the categories below, my desire isn't to provide a complete list of recommendations but to introduce you to the types of resources.

If you want specific suggestions, I encourage you to check out **deeperChristian.com/bibleresources**, a page I keep updated with my favorite recommendations, tools, and resources for studying the Bible.

---

1. USE A GOOD "STUDY" BIBLE

What I mean is probably different than what you are thinking. Rather than buying a typical "study Bible" (where there are study notes below the biblical text), I suggest you create your own "study" Bible — while you read and study the Bible, write your own notes, cross-references, and other helpful insights in the margins.

> **The Bible, the whole Bible, and nothing but the Bible is the religion of Christ's church.**
>
> Leonard Ravenhill

Here are a couple of things to consider having in your own "study" Bible:

- **A word-for-word Bible translation.** When you study, you want to get as close to the original languages as possible. So start with a solid word-for-word translation.[29] I love to use the Legacy Standard Bible (LSB), but here are a few others I'd recommend: New American Standard Bible (NASB95), English Standard Version (ESV), Lexham English Bible (LEB), Modern English Version (MEV), King James Version (KJV), and New King James Version (NKJV). I also enjoy having the Amplified Bible nearby as a reference tool.

- **A Bible *without* study notes or commentary**

at the bottom of the page. I've noticed that people who use traditional "study Bibles," with commentary notes at the bottom of the page, lean on those notes rather than doing their own study. While these notes can be helpful for quick reference, they often distract, and people can unintentionally give the notes the same priority and authority as the actual words of Scripture. My suggestion is to have your resources separate from your Bible (except for cross-references and translation notes that may come with a standard Bible).

- **Invest a little extra and get better paper quality.** Don't buy a pew Bible or a cheap paperback version — they fall apart too quickly. A Bible with good paper and a cover that will endure doesn't have to be expensive (I love imitation leather over the real stuff, and it's far cheaper).

- **Wide margins** (or a journaling Bible). While some people desire a nice "keepsake" Bible, I suggest you get a Bible you can use, mark up, and fill with notes. I can trace my spiritual journey through the various Bibles I've used. Typically I have to replace my Bible every couple of years because of use — and reviewing my notes reminds me of all God has done and taught me throughout my spiritual life. So a Bible with larger margins can be beneficial if you plan to write in it.

2. BIBLE DICTIONARIES & ENCYCLOPEDIAS

A Bible dictionary is like Webster's but focuses specifically on words and terms in Scripture.

When you come to a word or phrase, it is important to understand what it means (how often have you skipped over terms like *propitiation* or *justification* because you didn't know what they meant?).

Here are two examples of entries of the word "cistern," the first from *Easton's Bible Dictionary* and the second from *Holman Illustrated Bible Dictionary*.

> **CISTERN** — the rendering of a Hebrew word bor, which means a receptacle for water conveyed to it; distinguished from beer, which denotes a place where water rises on the spot (Jer. 2:13; Prov. 5:15; Isa. 36:16), a fountain. Cisterns are frequently mentioned in Scripture. The scarcity of springs in Palestine made it necessary to collect rain-water in reservoirs and cisterns (Num. 21:22). (See WELL.
>
> Empty cisterns were sometimes used as prisons (Jer. 38:6; Lam. 3:53; Ps. 40:2; 69:15). The "pit" into which Joseph was cast (Gen. 37:24) was a beer or dry well. There are numerous remains of ancient cisterns in all parts of Palestine.[30]

> *CISTERN* Translation of a Hebrew term that means "hole," "pit," or more often "well." The difference between "cistern" and "well" often is not apparent. The innumerable cisterns, wells, and pools that exist in Palestine are evidence of the efforts of ancient people to supplement the natural water supply. The cistern of Palestine was usually a bottle or pear-shaped reservoir into which water could drain from a roof, tunnel, or courtyard. The porous limestone out of which the cisterns were dug allowed much of the water put into the cistern to escape. After 1300 B.C. cisterns began to be plastered, which resulted in a more efficient system of water storage. The mouth of a cistern was sometimes finished and covered with a stone. Some cisterns have been found with a crude filter to trap debris. The

biblical writers revealed that cisterns were used for purposes other than holding water. Joseph was placed in a "broken" cistern by his brothers (Gen. 37:20–29). The prophet Jeremiah was imprisoned in the cistern of Malchijah, King Zedekiah's son (Jer. 38:6 NASB). In Jer. 14 the pagan gods were symbolized as broken cisterns that could not hold water. Cisterns also served as convenient dumping places for corpses (Jer. 41:7, 9). See Waterworks; Wells.[31]

That's a lot of information, but reading through a Bible dictionary will help you understand how a word is used throughout Scripture and often give you further passages to track down on the word or topic.

3. CONCORDANCES

Most Bibles have a simple concordance in the back. A Bible concordance is a list of all the verses in Scripture using a specific word. These are specific to your Bible translation and can be helpful to quickly find a reference for a verse when you can only remember a word or two.

An exhaustive concordance is the expanded version of the one in the back of your Bible — usually containing all the references, not just the more popular verses.

When considering a concordance, note that there are two kinds: those based on English and those based on the original languages (i.e., Hebrew and Greek). For example, if you want to look up all the verses containing the word "love," an English concordance will show you every reference in which the English word "love" is used, but it often does not clarify which of the four Greek words for love is used. Since the Greek gives a different nuance to each word, it can be helpful to search an exhaustive concordance that separates the word "love" into the four primary words in Greek (*agapē, phileō, eros, storge*).

Online or digital concordances are the best (often using Strong's Exhaustive Concordance) because they allow for quick searching without having to flip pages and jump back and forth between the concordance and your Bible.

4. CROSS REFERENCES

You can find cross-references in many Bibles as a center column. Cross-references suggest other Bible passages that have to do with similar words or topics.

Whether or not your Bible has cross-references, I encourage you to create your own. When you encounter a passage linked to another in theme, topic, phrase, etc., write the reference in your Bible. I suggest going to both passages and writing the other reference so you have it in both places, creating a link between the two. That way, no matter which verse you come across later, you have a reference to the other one.

My cross-references are one of the few things I copy over when I get a new Bible — I love the links (cross-references) connecting words, concepts, topics, and phrases I have discovered over the years.

For example, in my Bible, I wrote the reference "Deut. 6:5" next to 2 Kings 23:25, which says of King Josiah, "Before him there was no king like him who turned to the LORD with all his heart and with all his soul and with all his might, according to all the law of Moses; nor did any like him arise after him." This passage quotes what the Jews call "The Shema" (Deuteronomy 6:4–5): "Hear, O Israel! The LORD is our God, the LORD is one! You shall love the LORD your God with all your heart and with all your soul and with all your might." And to help give me an example of someone who lived "the greatest commandment," I put the reference "2 Kgs 23:25" next to Deuteronomy 6:4–5.

If I turn to Deuteronomy 6:4–5 in my Bible, I'll also see the references for: Matthew 22:36–40, Mark 12:28–31, Luke 10:25–37, Ecclesiastes 12:13 — and the list keeps growing.

5. BIBLE ATLAS (MAPS)

A Bible atlas has become an indispensable tool in my Bible study. Don't overlook the geography of the Bible — incredible insights are found when you see where the Bible happened.

While some Bibles may have a few maps in the back, a Bible atlas is an expanded resource with dozens (sometimes hundreds) of maps, charts, and graphics to help you understand the significance of geography in Scripture. Often broken up into locations, books of the Bible, or Biblical accounts, a Bible atlas is handy to look up locations, topography, and distances as you study God's Word.

Also consider aiding your understanding of Bible geography by going on an Israel Bible Study Tour. Unlike a tourist trip, a Bible study tour allows you to walk the land, experience the culture, and study the Bible on location with like-hearted believers. Learn more at **deeperChristian.com/israel** and consider joining me on the next study tour I lead...yes, this is a shameless plug — but the trip will open up the Bible unlike you've ever seen and will profoundly impact your life. I'd love for you to join me!

OTHER HELPFUL TOOLS AND RESOURCES

BIBLE HANDBOOKS

A Bible handbook can be a great tool to help you gain a quick understanding of a book of the Bible (or a section of Scripture). Handbooks typically explain background information on the author, audience, and provide an overview of the purpose, main structure, key passages, and important topics of each book of the Bible.

My favorite handbook is *Talk Thru the Bible* (by Wilkinson and Boa). This is one of the few Bible resources (along with a Bible atlas) I love to have a print copy of to flip through and see the charts.

LEXICONS

A lexicon is a dictionary for Hebrew and Greek words. They are more academic and technical than the Bible dictionaries mentioned above, often requiring a basic understanding of that language. These dictionaries are organized alphabetically in Hebrew or Greek and can be extremely helpful in understanding the original languages.

GRAMMARS (FOR HEBREW AND GREEK)

If you are interested in learning Hebrew (Old Testament) or Koine Greek (New Testament), you'll need what is called a "grammar." Some good online classes and book suggestions are available on the recommended resource page online (*deeperChristian.com/bibleresources*).

COMMENTARIES

You may have wondered why I've waited till now to

mention commentaries. I love a good commentary, but I've noticed far too many students of the Word rely almost exclusively upon commentaries and fail to actually study for themselves — they merely glean insights from others who have studied the Bible.

Commentaries are a way to ask someone, scholar or not, what a passage means. While their perspective may give insight or press on something that helps you wrestle with the text more deeply, they are still not a substitute for Scripture itself.

You must remember that **the Bible is its own best commentary**!

Every commentary is someone's study and interpretation of the Word. While these can be helpful (especially with understanding culture, history, and original languages), my suggestion is to wrestle through the Biblical text yourself and use commentaries later in your study, so you don't rely upon their conclusions.

In other words, don't use commentaries to shortchange your own study of Scripture; use them to augment and deepen your own study.

As you look for commentaries, note there are two different styles of commentaries — what I will call "sermonic" and "academic."

A sermonic commentary is typically a "commentary" comprised of someone's sermon, whether the actual transcript or a written version of the sermon (for example, commentaries compiled from the sermons of Charles Spurgeon, Martyn Lloyd-Jones, or Stephen Manley).

An academic commentary is often written by professors and scholars analyzing the passage in light of original language, grammar, structure, history, culture, geography, etc. These read differently than a sermon and sometimes require a basic grasp of Hebrew or Greek. Often more analytical, these types of commentaries usually don't give answers or conclusions as much as they help you understand the text so you can come to your own conclusions.

While sermonic commentaries can be beneficial for your personal devotional and spiritual life, if you plan to use commentaries, use academic ones in your study. You can use sermonic commentaries later in the study to deepen, augment, or discover potential missing concepts.

One final note about commentaries. Most people use commentaries from scholars from their own theological traditions. But it is helpful to gather a few different commentaries from a variety of theological perspectives (i.e., Reformed, Arminian, Pentecostal, etc.) or denominations (i.e., Baptist, Methodist, Presbyterian, Lutheran, Wesleyan, etc.) so that you can better understand the tension points and come to an informed decision based on a variety of opinions and perspectives rather than just one scholar's conclusions. Though this approach takes more time to read and wrestle through, it helps you better understand the nuances and differing views of a passage.

IN A NUTSHELL...

- Remember, the Bible is its own best commentary...and you should use the Bible to interpret the Bible.

- If you use commentaries, use them later in your study process, so it gives you time to wrestle with the text before you seek someone's opinions,

- Lean toward academic commentaries over sermonic commentaries for your Bible study.

- Use a variety of commentaries to see perspectives, insights, and tension points.

- While a commentary series may look good on your shelf, not all commentaries within a series may be the best option for a particular book of the Bible. Rather than buy an entire series, pick and choose good commentaries for the book you are studying from different series. To find good commentaries on a specific book, consider using a resource like *An Annotated Guide to Biblical Resources for Ministry* by David Bauer, *The Pastor's Library* by Robert Yost, or *bestcommentaries.com* — all three give reviews of the best commentaries for each book of the Bible.

That being said, here are a few commentary series I've found particularly helpful (more suggestions are available at deeperChristian.com/bibleresources).

- *The New International Commentary of the New Testament*

- *The New International Greek Testament Commentary*

- *Word Biblical Commentary* (requires a basic understanding of Hebrew or Greek)

- *New American Commentary*

- *Pillar New Testament Commentary*

- *Wiersbe's "Be" Series*

ONLINE BIBLE STUDY TOOLS

Digital resources have transformed my personal Bible study time and have come in handy when traveling, quickly searching for something, or being able to copy/paste and follow ideas and concepts without having to turn pages.

Over the years, I've spent a lot of time on BlueLetterBible.org, but eventually saved my money and upgraded to Logos Bible Software.

If you're starting out, I suggest you use a free online resource like BlueLetterBible. It is amazingly comprehensive for being free, and its tools get better every year. If you'd like a simple overview of how to use BlueLetterBible in your study, check out the free tutorial I put together at deeperChristian.com/saturationbook.

LOGOS BIBLE SOFTWARE

I've tried nearly all the major Bible study software over the years, and Logos is by far my favorite. I use it almost every day and what it allows me to do boggles my mind. Don't get me wrong, it's expensive, but personally, it's worth every penny.

My brother is a fantastic plumber. Over the years, he has spent thousands of dollars buying the tools and equipment he needed to do his job. Similarly, Bible study is one of my main focuses in ministry and one of my passions. So while friends have scoffed at the money I spent on Logos, for me, it's like my brother buying the necessary tools for his job.

Funny note: years ago, my roommate got engaged at the same time I bought Logos, and we both spent the same amount of money that month—he bought a ring, and I bought Bible software. I guess we both had different priorities, haha.

———————

For most people who study the Bible, Logos is overkill—and I think 90% of people who study the Bible would find everything they need in a free tool like blueletterbible.org. But if you want to take your study to another level, have access to great digital resources at a discounted price, and have everything indexed and searchable, Logos is what I recommend.

If I may geek out for another moment—one of the other reasons I love Logos, besides its powerful tools and features, is that I have the books by some of my favorite people available and searchable. I used to spend hours searching for quotes by Charles Spurgeon, A.W. Tozer, Andrew Murray, Oswald Chambers, the Puritans, and countless others. Now I have all their books in my software and can quickly search based on a word, topic, phrase, or Bible passage.

I have more information about Logos Bible Software, including a discount code (which gives you a discount off the cost and also helps support the ministry of deeperChristian in the process, at no additional cost to you) at deeperChristian.com/bibleresources.

GUIDED OBSERVATION STUDY

*The one marvelous secret of a holy life
lies not in imitating Jesus, but in letting
the perfections of Jesus manifest
themselves in my mortal flesh.
Sanctification is "Christ in you."...
Sanctification is not drawing from Jesus
the power to be holy; it is drawing from
Jesus the holiness that was manifested
in Him, and He manifests it in me.*
Oswald Chambers

Welcome to your first guided study. These guided studies are designed to walk you step-by-step through the process of Bible study and help you practice the concepts throughout this book.

Since we spend the majority of our study time in the observation stage, where we peruse, pray, and ponder a passage, I want us to practically work through the process of observing a text. Again, the longer we spend time thinking and examining the passage, the more we will discover. Let me give you a classic example to show you what I mean.

Look at the following graphic. How many squares do you see?

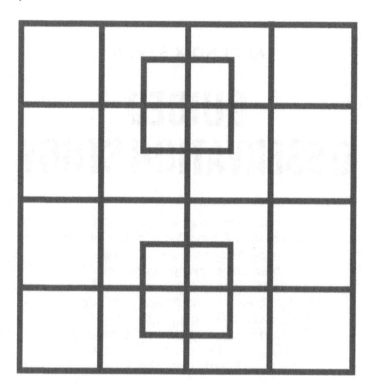

Did you find 18? More than 25?

Perhaps surprisingly, there are 40 squares hidden in the graphic. See the end of this appendix to discover all 40 squares.

It's an illuminating lesson; the more you observe, the more you discover. This is also true with Bible study.

Remember that though the observation stage takes the longest of the four steps, there is no hurry. The goal of Saturation is to know Jesus and be transformed by truth — and we do that all throughout the process — so there is no rush.

While you could work through this guided study in a single sitting, I encourage you to go through this observation process over the next seven days. If you rush through the practical exercises below, you will have a good understanding of how to observe a text but miss the importance of saturating in it. Like meat in a marinade or a good cup of French Press coffee, take the time to soak in the passage. Again, we are not in a rush.

FOCUS

We are going to examine Ephesians 1:4, within the context of Ephesians 1:3–14.

BEFORE EACH DAY

Before you begin each day, start with prayer. Ask God to prepare your heart and give you insight into His Word. Invite Him into the study and declare your desire to know (ginōskō) Him more and be transformed by truth.

DAY 1

When we observe a passage, the best place to start is reading and re-reading the passage. In your Bible, read Ephesians 1:1–14 a couple of times.

What is the "big picture" of what Paul is saying? What is a summary of these first fourteen verses of Ephesians?

Read Ephesians 1:4 in a variety of translations. As you read through each translation, note any similarities, differences, and initial insights you gleaned from the passage. Consider writing the verse down on a notecard (in your primary translation) and carry it with you throughout the day — pull it out, read the verse, and ponder what it says.

Today, don't worry about doing anything specific; just read and re-read the text below.

> **NASB** – ...just as He chose us in Him before the foundation of the world, that we would be holy and blameless before Him. In love...

> **ESV** – ...even as he chose us in him before the foundation of the world, that we should be holy and blameless before him. In love...

> **NKJV** – ...just as He chose us in Him before the foundation of the world, that we should be holy and without blame before Him in love...

> **NIV**–For he chose us in him before the creation of the world to be holy and blameless in his sight. In love...

> **NLT**–Even before he made the world, God loved us and chose us in Christ to be holy and without fault in his eyes.

> **LSB** – ...just as He chose us in Him before the foundation of the world, that we would be holy and blameless before Him in love...

> **AMP**–Even as [in His love] He chose us [actually picked us out for Himself as His own] in Christ before the foundation of the world, that we should be holy (consecrated and set apart for Him) and blameless in His sight, even above reproach, before Him in love.

DAY 2

In the context of our passage (Ephesians 1:3–14), Paul gives an overview of the blessings we have in God. Every spiritual blessing is found in Christ Jesus because God is a blessed God who can't help but bless those He loves (see Ephesians 1:3).

After the general overview in verse three, Paul gets into the actual blessings in 1:4–14. While this is not a comprehensive list (there are many others listed throughout Scripture), Paul is explaining the "riches of His grace which He lavished on us" (1:7–8).

While I encourage you to eventually study all the blessings found in Ephesians 1, we want to focus on the first one Paul mentions in 1:4.

One of the aspects of Saturation is to continually keep a passage in mind and soak within it throughout the day. I encourage you to go back and read the entire section (Ephesians 1:3–14) in your Bible every day this week and focus specifically on verse four (read and reflect upon the verse over and over).

Examine Ephesians 1:4 and make a list of as many observations as you can find. Again, observations are anything you see in the text and key questions that help you dig deeper. Here are a few simple questions to get you started (consider using the "what to look for" document in Appendix 5 for additional questions to ask):

- What are the main keywords in the passage?

- How would you summarize or write the passage in your own words?

- What is the key action in the passage? Who is doing the action (God, Paul, us, or someone else)?

- Where does the key action take place?

- Does Paul mention a time element for the main action (when it took place)?

- What is the purpose or result of the main action? Why is God doing the main action?

Take the passage with you throughout the day, reflect upon it, make observations, and ask God to give you wisdom and insight into it.

DAY 3

One of the main keywords in the passage is the verb "chose." Do a word study on what this word means in its original language (Greek). For a video tutorial on how to do a word study, visit deeperChristian.com/ saturationbook.

Here is a summary of the word study I did:

CHOSE

- Greek: *eklegomai*

- Parsing: Verb, Aorist, Middle, Indicative, 3rd Person, Singular

  » Aorist Tense: often translated in the past tense but typically signifies a focus on the action and less on "when" it took place. In other words, don't worry about when it happened; focus on what happened.

  » Indicative: a simple statement of fact

- Etymology: from two root words: *ek* (from, out of) + *legō* (to say, speak, call)

- Biblical Usage: to pick out, choose, to pick or choose out for one's self

- Occurs 22x in 20 verses in the NT

  » Key passages: Luke 6:13; 9:35; 14:7; John 15:16; Acts 1:2

Throughout the day, consider the concept of God choosing us. Reflect upon the word, its meaning, and look up key passages and see how the word is used in those other passages. What additional observations, insights, and thoughts do you have?

DAY 4

Yesterday we spent time pondering the concept of God choosing us. Let's continue the reflection by examining *where* it takes place.

Notice Paul says that God chose us IN Him, speaking of Jesus. We are chosen in Christ! Paul uses the phrase "in Christ" throughout His writing to discuss the Christian's position. Just in the first three chapters of Ephesians, Paul uses a variety of that phrase thirty times (e.g., in Him, in Whom, in Christ).

We are not chosen apart from Christ — it is not because of who we are or what we have done (see Ephesians 2:8–10 and John 15:16). It is all because of Jesus, and we solely find our hope, salvation, security, joy, and life in Him. Our position is IN Christ.

There are so many promises and benefits of being IN Jesus! Though this is not a complete list, read through it and spend the day reflecting on what it means to be chosen IN Christ Jesus.

WHEN WE ARE IN CHRIST...

- We will bear much fruit (John 15:5)

- We will be made alive to God (Romans 6:11; 1 Corinthians 15:31)

- There will be no more condemnation hanging over our lives (Romans 8:1)

- We will be made free from the law of sin and death (Romans 8:2)

- Nothing will be able to separate us from the love of God (Romans 8:38–39)

- We will have access to the Wisdom, the Righteousness, the Sanctification, and the Redemption of God (1 Corinthians 1:30)

- All the Promises of God will be "Yes" and "Amen" to us (2 Corinthians 1:20)

- Our spiritual lives will be established and anointed (2 Corinthians 1:21)

- We will be led forth in triumph (2 Corinthians 2:14)

- He will diffuse through our lives the fragrance of His knowledge in every place (2 Corinthians 2:14)

- The veil that shrouds our spiritual sight will be taken away (2 Corinthians 3:14)

- We will become new creations; all things will become new (2 Corinthians 5:17)

- The complexities of life will be made simple (2 Corinthians 11:3)

- We will from henceforth live by the power of God (2 Corinthians 13:4, Ephesians 1:19–20)

- We will have an astounding liberty to now do that which is right (Galatians 2:4)

- We will become sons of God (Galatians 3:26)

- We will be blessed with every spiritual blessing in the heavenly places (Ephesians 1:3)

- We will be chosen to be holy and without blame (Ephesians 1:4)

- We will obtain an inheritance (Ephesians 1:11)

- We will be made to sit with Him in heavenly places (Ephesians 2:6)

- We will be made to know the exceeding riches of His grace in His kindness toward us (Ephesians 2:7)

- We will have works prepared beforehand for us to walk in (Ephesians 2:10)

- We will be brought intimately near into His very presence, and we will have boldness and confidence in our approach unto His Throne (Ephesians 2:13; 3:12)

- We will become the very temple of the Lord, the very dwelling place of God (Ephesians 2:21–21)

- We, the Gentiles, will become fellow heirs and partakers of the promises (Ephesians 3:6)

- We will know His Great Mystery that has been hidden for ages and generations (Ephesians 3:9–11; Colossians 1:26–27)

- We will have power to rejoice (Philippians 3:3)

- We will have a prize set before us of the upward call of God (Philippians 3:14)

- We will have access into all the fulness of God (Colossians 1:19; 2:9)

- We will be clothed in His Perfection (Colossians 1:28)

- All the treasures of wisdom and knowledge will be made available to us (Colossians 2:3)

- We will abound in thanksgiving (Colossians 2:7)

- We will be made complete (Colossians 2:10)

- We will be circumcised from the sins of the flesh (Colossians 2:11)

- We will have the promise of Life (2 Timothy 1:1)

- We will be given a holy calling (2 Timothy 1:9)

- We will be supplied an empowering grace (2 Timothy 1:9; 2 Timothy 2:1)

- We will have faith and love (2 Timothy 1:13)

- We will have salvation (2 Timothy 2:10)

- There will be no more darkness (1 John 1:5)

- The Love of God will be perfected in us (1 John 2:5)

- We will not be ashamed before Him at His coming (1 John 2:28)

- We will purify ourselves just as He is pure (1 John 3:3)

- We will not sin (1 John 3:6)

- Anything we ask according to His will, He will hear us (1 John 5:14)

- We will know Him (1 John 5:20)

DAY 5

We are chosen IN Christ! Let's continue the reflection by observing *when* it took place. Paul says that it happened "before the foundation of the world."

The Greek word for "foundation" is **katabolē** which gives the idea of "laying down" or creating a foundation. Interestingly, of the eleven times it is used in the New Testament, it is always used in reference to the world, except once in Hebrews 11:11 when it refers to Sarah being able to conceive by faith (**katabolē** is translated here as "conceive").

The Greek word for "world" is **kosmos** (where we get the English word "cosmos"). It has a few meanings like "world," "order," or could refer to humanity or world affairs. But every time it is used in conjunction with the word katabolē (foundation), the context specifically refers to the created world.

Throughout the day, make a list of observations and implications of what it means for God to choose you BEFORE the "foundation of the world."

To aid your reflection and observation, read Genesis 1:1–2:3; Jeremiah 1:4–5; Matthew 25:34; John 1:1–3; Colossians 1:13–20.

DAY 6

Paul explains the reason why God chose us before the foundation of the world is so "that we would be holy and blameless before Him."

Do a study on the words "holy" and "blameless." Throughout the day, consider God's desire for your life to be holy and blameless. What additional observations, biblical insights, and thoughts do you have on these two topics?

Here is a summary of the word studies I did:

HOLY

- Greek: *hagios*

- Etymology: comes from the idea of "pure, chaste, clear" and from the Hebrew concept of being set apart and unlike the world

- Biblical Usage: most holy thing; saint; used to describe the Spirit of God (i.e., Holy Spirit)

- Occurs 233x in the NT and 627x in the OT

    » Key passages: Exodus 3:5; 15:11; Luke 1:49; 2:23; Romans 12:1;

    » Interesting to note that while Paul usually uses the word for the "Holy Spirit" and "saints," he also describes as holy: Scripture (Romans 1:2), Law (Romans 7:12), root (Romans 11:16), kiss (Romans 16:16; 1 Corinthians 16:20; 2 Corinthians 13:12; 1 Thessalonians 5:26), the sanctuary of God (1 Corinthians 3:17; Ephesians 2:21), children (1 Corinthians 7:14), unmarried women (1 Corinthians 7:34), the Christian (Ephesians 1:4; Colossians 1:22, 3:12), apostles and prophets (Ephesians 3:5), the church (Ephesians 5:27), and God's calling (2 Timothy 1:9).

BLAMELESS

- Greek: *amōmos*

- Etymology: from two Greek words meaning *a* (without, no) + *mōmos* (blemish)–(i.e., without blemish)

- Biblical Usage: without blemish, faultless, blameless, without spot, unblameable

- Occurs 9x in the NT and 78x in OT

  » Passages: Ephesians 1:4, 5:27; Philippians 2:15; Colossians 1:22; Hebrews 9:14; 1 Peter 1:19; Jude 1:24; Revelation 14:5, 18:13

  » Important to note that this word is used of Jesus as the perfect sacrifice (Hebrews 9:14 and 1 Peter 1:19) and used throughout the Old Testament for how animals had to be for sacrifice (see Exodus 12:5). Interesting to consider this concept in light of Isaiah 53:7; John 1:29; Acts 8:32–35; Romans 8:29; 1 John 4:17, etc.

DAY 7

Go back and read Ephesians 1:1–14 and consider the significance of verse four in light of all the blessings Paul mentions. Is there any significance for Paul placing this one first?

Read through all your observations from the last seven days and write a summary statement of the observations for what Paul is saying about being chosen by God.

How many squares do you see? Answer: 40

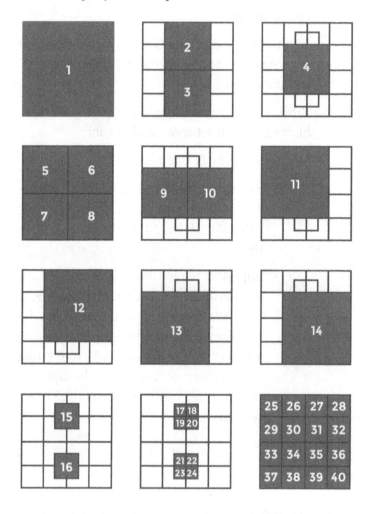

GUIDED PASSAGE STUDY

Acts 1:8

We are going to take the six-stage path mentioned in chapter 13 and walk through Acts 1:6–8, focusing specifically on verse eight.

Here are a few reminders before we jump into the study:

- There is no rush. Take your time throughout the study to think, review, and reflect upon the passage.

- Saturate in the passage and take the study with you throughout the day. Consider writing the verses on a notecard and carrying it with you to think, ask questions, make observations, etc.

- This study will likely take you a few days to go through (again, there is no pressure to rush). So before you start engaging with the passage each day:

» Start with prayer. Ask God to prepare your heart and give you insight into His Word. Invite Him into the study and declare your desire to know (ginōskō) Him more and be transformed by truth.

» Read the passage (Acts 1:6–8) multiple times and consider the larger context of Acts 1:1–11.

_____

For a printable version of this guided study, visit **deeperChristian.com/saturationbook**.

_____

WHAT YOU'LL NEED

1. **Bible**–I encourage you to have a physical Bible handy for these studies. While you could use online and digital resources, I've found reading and studying from a physical Bible changes the way I engage with the text. Use whatever primary translation you typically use (and if you are looking for a good translation, I encourage you to use a word-for-word translation such as: KJV, NKJV, NASB, LSB, ESV, CSB, etc.).

2. **Notebook or computer**–to record your observations and thoughts, use pen and paper, a computer or digital device, or a combination of both.

1. SELECT A PASSAGE

Ideally, we would select an entire book or long passage to study, but for the sake of this guided study, we will focus on Acts 1:8 and its surrounding context.

2. GET THE BIG PICTURE

The 30,000-foot view

2.1 – THE AUTHOR

Who wrote the book?

The author of Acts isn't explicitly mentioned, though in 1:1 he mentions, "The first account I composed, Theophilus, about all that Jesus began to do and teach..." If we search the Bible for "Theophilus," we discover it only appears twice (in Luke 1:3 and Acts 1:1). Based upon this and Christian tradition, we know Luke is the author of this two-volume book: Luke/Acts.

But what do we know about Luke? Read the following passages and record what you discover about him: Colossians 4:14; 2 Timothy 4:11; Philemon 1:24. Also consider the "we" passages in Acts, where it is presumed Luke joined Paul in his ministry: Acts 16:10–17; 20:5–21:18; 27:1–28:16.

For more consideration, read this paragraph taken from the Bible handbook *Talk Thru the Bible*:

> Luke may have been a Hellenistic Jew, but it is more likely that he was a Gentile (this would make him the only gentile contributor to the New Testament). In Colossians 4:10–14, Paul lists three fellow workers who are "of the circumcision" (Col. 4:10–11) and then includes Luke's name with two Gentiles (Col. 4:12–14). Luke's obvious skill with the Greek language and his phrase

"their own language" in Acts 1:19 also imply that he was not Jewish. It has been suggested that Luke may have been a Greek physician to a Roman family who at some point was set free and given Roman citizenship.... Tradition also says that Luke was from Syrian Antioch, remained unmarried, and died at the age of eighty-four.

Suggested dates for the writing of Acts range from A.D. 62 to the middle of the second century. Twentieth-century archaeological discoveries have strikingly confirmed the trustworthiness and precision of Luke as a historian and show that his work should be dated in the first century. Luke's perplexingly abrupt ending with Paul awaiting trial in Rome has led many to believe that Acts was completed prior to Paul's trial (A.D. 62). If it was written after this crucial event, why didn't Luke mention the outcome? Luke may have had a reason, but the simplest explanation of his silence is that Paul had not yet stood before Caesar. Acts gives no hint of the persecution under Nero (A.D. 64), Paul's death (A.D. 68), or the destruction of Jerusalem (A.D. 70).[32]

2.2 – THE AUDIENCE

Who was the author writing to?

Read Acts 1:1 and Luke 1:1–4.

Note that "Theophilus" is a Greek name meaning "friend of God." Many scholars presume Theophilus was the financial benefactor behind Luke's research and writing of the two-volume book of Luke/Acts.

2.3 – THE AUTHOR'S PURPOSE OF THE BOOK

What's the point?

Luke explains his two-volume book: "Many people have set out to write accounts about the events that have been fulfilled among us. They used the eyewitness reports circulating among us from the early disciples. Having carefully investigated everything from the beginning, I also have decided to write an accurate account for you, most honorable Theophilus, so you can be certain of the truth of everything you were taught" (Luke 1:1–4, NLT).

Though the book may have been originally intended for Theophilus, it was circulated with the other Gospel accounts within the Early Church.

Stephen Manley says this about Luke and Acts having the same focus:

> Luke's purpose for writing the Book of Acts is the same as his purpose for writing the Gospel of Luke, the truly former account.... Luke writes one book, not two. He has the same purpose, and he uses the same style and thrust in each volume. Thus, there is no way to grasp the Book of Acts without first understanding the flow from the Gospel of Luke. What is the theme? This is the proposition. There is a divine God who is acting in redemptive ways. Every story, every circumstance, every scene is about a God activity thing.[33]

2.4 – THE BACKGROUND

What's going on?

Acts 1 picks up where Luke 24 leaves off. Read Luke 24:1–12, 36–53, and Acts 1:1–11. Notice that Acts begins with a summary and greater explanation of what is recorded at the end of Luke. Consider using the other Gospel accounts for more details.

Summarize the background and the overall context for Acts 1:1–11.

2.5 – THE GENRE

What's the category?

The book of Acts is a historical account of what happened in the Early Church.

2.6 – OUTLINE OF THE PASSAGE

What is the structure?

Typically, we'd want to create an outline of the entire book, but since our focus is on a smaller passage, read through Acts 1:1–11 multiple times and break it into several key sections. Make sure you name (title) each section.[34]

2.7 – MAJOR THEMES AND TOPICS

What's it all about?

The major theme of Acts is the movement and action of the Holy Spirit in the lives of the apostles and members of the Early Church.

Read through our passage (Acts 1:1–11) and record any repeated themes, topics, words, or phrases.

3. PRAY

Before engaging with the text, ask the Holy Spirit to give you insight, wisdom, and understanding into His Word.

I love using Ephesians 1:17–18 as a Bible study prayer — "God, give me a spirit of wisdom and revelation in the knowledge of You. I pray that the eyes of my heart may be enlightened..."

Take the time before every study to:

- Consecrate your heart and mind
- Surrender your life and will
- Ask for wisdom, insight, and grace to understand
- Commit to obey His Word regardless of how difficult it may be
- Declare that you desire to know Him (not just information) and that you long for the Word to sanctify and transform your life so that you might be conformed to the image of Christ
- Ask for His involvement, grace, and enablement not only in the study but to live it out

4. READ IN LIGHT OF THE BIG PICTURE

Now that we've walked through the "big picture" of Acts, take the time to read through the entire book. While this will take some time, it will be helpful to see our passage (Acts 1:1–11) in light of the entire book. As you read, consider how the book illuminates, explains, and deepens our passage (and visa versa).

5. CHOOSE A SECTION OF VERSES TO STUDY

If we were to study the entire book of Acts, we'd start with the introduction (1:1–3) and move through the book section by section. However, for the rest of this guided study, we will narrow our focus of study to Acts 1:6–8, specifically verse eight.

6. ASK THE FOUR QUESTIONS

6.1 – WHAT DOES THE TEXT SAY? (OBSERVATION)

Remember, the observation stage will take the longest amount of time. Don't feel rushed working through this section but take several days (or weeks) to work through the observations.

6.1.1 – Start with reading Acts 1:6–8 in a variety of translations. As you do, notice differences between translations and key words that stand out to you.

> **NASB**–So when they had come together, they were asking Him, saying, "Lord, is it at this time You are restoring the kingdom to Israel?" He said to them, "It is not for you to know times or epochs which the Father has fixed by His own authority; but you will receive power when the Holy Spirit has come upon you; and you shall be My witnesses both in Jerusalem, and in all Judea and Samaria, and even to the remotest part of the earth."

> **ESV**–So when they had come together, they asked him, "Lord, will you at this time restore the kingdom to Israel?" He said to them, "It is not for you to know times or seasons that the Father has fixed by his own authority. But you will receive power when the Holy Spirit has come upon you, and you will be my witnesses in Jerusalem and in all Judea and Samaria, and to the end of the earth."

> **NKJV**–Therefore, when they had come together, they asked Him, saying, "Lord, will You at this time restore the kingdom to Israel?" And He said to them, "It is not for you to know times or seasons which the Father has put in His own authority. But you shall receive power when the Holy Spirit has

come upon you; and you shall be witnesses to Me in Jerusalem, and in all Judea and Samaria, and to the end of the earth."

NIV-Then they gathered around him and asked him, "Lord, are you at this time going to restore the kingdom to Israel?" He said to them: "It is not for you to know the times or dates the Father has set by his own authority. But you will receive power when the Holy Spirit comes on you; and you will be my witnesses in Jerusalem, and in all Judea and Samaria, and to the ends of the earth."

NLT-So when the apostles were with Jesus, they kept asking him, "Lord, has the time come for you to free Israel and restore our kingdom?" He replied, "The Father alone has the authority to set those dates and times, and they are not for you to know. But you will receive power when the Holy Spirit comes upon you. And you will be my witnesses, telling people about me everywhere — in Jerusalem, throughout Judea, in Samaria, and to the ends of the earth."

LSB-So when they had come together, they were asking Him, saying, "Lord, is it at this time You are restoring the kingdom to Israel?" But He said to them, "It is not for you to know times or seasons which the Father has set by His own authority; but you will receive power when the Holy Spirit has come upon you; and you shall be My witnesses both in Jerusalem, and in all Judea and Samaria, and even to the end of the earth."

AMP-So when they were assembled, they asked Him, "Lord, is this the time when You will reestablish the kingdom and restore it to Israel?" He said to them, "It is not for you to become acquainted with and know what time brings [the things and events of time and their definite periods] or fixed years and seasons (their critical niche in time), which the Father has appointed (fixed and reserved) by His own choice and authority and personal power. But you shall receive power (ability, efficiency, and might) when the Holy Spirit has come upon you, and you shall be My witnesses in Jerusalem and all Judea and Samaria and to the ends (the very bounds) of the earth."

6.1.2 – Examine verse six and, in your own words, summarize the central question the disciples are asking Jesus.

> **Acts 1:6** – *So when they had come together, they were asking Him, saying, "Lord, is it at this time You are restoring the kingdom to Israel?"*

Consider these quotes from three commentaries on this passage:

> "They thought Christ would restore the kingdom to Israel, that is, that he would make the nation of the Jews as great and considerable among the nations as it was in the days of David and Solomon, of Asa and Jehoshaphat; that, as Shiloh, he would restore the scepter to Judah, and the lawgiver; whereas Christ came to set up his own kingdom, and that a kingdom of heaven, not to restore the kingdom to Israel, an earthly kingdom."[35]

> "Once we read the disciples' question against this [Old Testament prophetic background — Ezekiel 36–37; Isaiah 49:5–6] , we realize that it is a legitimate question asked by Israelites in the presence of the resurrected Messiah — Israelites who have particular expectations about the future and who are now being confronted with that future. This background sheds great light on Jesus' response as well. The Lord does not rebuke the disciples for asking the question. He tells them that

they do not or cannot know the time in familiar terms; only the Father knows the exact time. He redirects their question to the more important issue that focuses the disciples on a different idea of time. The disciples are thinking in regard to the consummation, the final establishment of the kingdom. They are also likely thinking of a decisive event. But Jesus directs them away from a specific day and instead focuses on the situation that exists as a result of his resurrection. The kingdom is being restored and will continue to be restored through the coming of the promised Holy Spirit, who will empower the disciples. The restoration begins now."[36]

"Israel at this time was under the political domination of Rome. Most Jews were unhappy with this situation and longed for the time that God would sovereignly intervene in fulfillment of the prophetic texts and remove these impure and arrogant Gentiles from power. The nation took matters into their own hands in A.D. 66 and inaugurated a war with the Roman forces that eventually led to the destruction of Jerusalem and the temple. It appears that the disciples still did not completely understand the nature of this phase of the kingdom plan that Jesus was inaugurating. In fairness to them, however, we need to realize that they had not yet received the indwelling presence of the Holy Spirit. After Pentecost, there was no more misunderstanding about this issue."[37]

What insight into the cultural context do these quotes give you into the mindset of the disciples?

Many scholars point out that the disciples were asking a cultural question. Because the Roman Empire had taken over the known world, the Jews during Jesus' day thought that when the Messiah came, He would free Israel from the Roman bondage and restore the nation to the glory days of David and Solomon. While the question is not bad, Jesus shifts their focus away from the political to the spiritual (in verses 7–8).

For additional insight into this cultural perspective, consider our passage in light of John 6:14–15.

6.1.3 – Verse eight becomes the focal point of the entire section. Jesus, in essence, is answering the question the disciples should have been asking but didn't. Let's begin to observe the text from a variety of angles.

Start with making a list of observations you see in the verse and write down any questions you have.

> **Acts 1:8 (ESV) – *But you will receive power when the Holy Spirit has come upon you, and you will be my witnesses in Jerusalem and in all Judea and Samaria, and to the end of the earth.***

6.1.4 – The Holy Spirit is the central focus of verse eight. The power and witness come as a result of the Holy Spirit "coming upon you." What do you know about the Holy Spirit? Make a list of everything you know about the Holy Spirit; use the verses below for additional help and insight.

- Genesis 1:2; Exodus 31:1–11; Psalm 139:1–24; Isaiah 11:1–16; Jeremiah 31:31–34; Ezekiel 36:26–27; 37:1–14; Joel 2:28–29; Matthew 3:11–17; 28:19–20; Luke 2:25–35; 4:18; 11:11–13; 24:49–53; John 3:1–4:26; 6:60–66; 7:37–39; 14:1–16:33; 20:19–25; Acts 2:1–4; 2:14–39; 4:5–12; 6:1–15; 10:17–11:30; 15:6–29; 19:1–10; Romans 5:1–5; 7:6; 8:1–30; 1 Corinthians 2:1–16; 3:5–17; 6:11, 19; 12:1–31; 2 Corinthians 1:15–2:2; 3:1–18; 5:1–8;

6:1–10; 13:11–14; Galatians 3:1–4:7; 5:1–26; 6:6–10; Ephesians 1:3–14; 2:18–22; 3:14–21; 5:15–21; 6:10–20; 1 Thessalonians 1:2–10; 1 Timothy 3:14–4:5; 2 Timothy 1:6–14; Titus 3:1–8; Hebrews 3:7–15; 6:1–8; 9:6-15; James 4:1–6; 1 Peter 1:1–12; 2 Peter 1:21; 1 John 2:20, 25–27; 3:24–4:16; 5:6–13.

6.1.5 – Word studies are important as they give you insight and depth into the meaning of a passage (the linguistic context). During your study, you can either look up any word you don't know or determine the main keywords in the passage and focus on those. In verse eight, there are two keywords we need to define: *power* and *witness*. Two additional word studies that could be helpful to examine (as they are the main verbs in the passage) are *you shall receive* and *you shall be*.

For a tutorial on how to do word studies in a free online resource like blueletterbible.org, visit **deeperChristian.com/saturationbook**.

POWER

- Greek word: ***dynamis***
- Definition: strength, power, ability
- Found 120x in NT
- Translated (in KJV) as: power (77x), mighty work (11x), strength (7x), miracle (7x), might (4x), virtue (3x), mighty (2x)

Read through a variety of the 120 places the word *dynamis* shows up in the New Testament (giving specific focus to the verses in Acts, as it is our book of focus) and make a list of insights and observations you discover about how this word is used. For example, I notice that dynamis is often used as the type of power that is physically seen or demonstrated (for example: miracles) — in contrast to an inner or hidden strength/power.

WITNESS

- Greek word: *martys*

- Definition: a witness

- Vine's Dictionary: where English gets its word "martyr" (one who bears "witness" by his death); denotes "one who can or does [declare] what he has seen or heard or knows"

- Found 34x in NT

- Translated (in KJV) as: witness (29x), martyr (3x), record (2x)

Read through a variety of the 34 places the word *martys* shows up in the New Testament (giving specific focus to the verses in Acts, as it is our book of focus) and make a list of insights and observations you discover about how this word is used. For example, I notice while this word can be used for someone who dies for their faith (what we typically think of when we hear the word "martyr"), it is also used for those who strongly believe something and stand resolutely for it.

YOU SHALL RECEIVE/YOU SHALL BE

It is often important to examine the main verbs of a passage, as verbs drive the action in a sentence. In Acts 1:8 we have two main verbs (*you shall receive* and *you shall be*). Even if you don't know Greek or grammar, looking at the "parsing" (grammatical parts) of a verb can help you determine what is going on in in the passage.

You shall receive (Greek: *lambanō*)

- Speech: Verb

- Tense: Future *(this will happen in the future)*

- Voice: Middle

- Mood: Indicative *(a simple statement of fact)*

- Person: 2nd Person

- Number: Plural *(the entire group, not a specific individual)*

You shall be (Greek: *eimi*)

- Speech: Verb

- Tense: Future *(this will happen in the future)*

- Voice: Middle

- Mood: Indicative *(a simple statement of fact)*

- Person: 2nd Person

- Number: Plural *(the entire group, not a specific individual)*

Notice both of these main verbs have the same tense, voice, mood, person, and number. Jesus is saying that when the Holy Spirit comes (in the future — which we know is at Pentecost in Acts 2) upon the group ("plural"–speaking of the group, not an individual), they will receive power and be witnesses (a simple statement of fact — this isn't a possibility but a certainty).

Also note there is seemingly a third verb in the passage "has come upon." But further investigation into its parsing, we discover that the "mood" of the Greek word **eperchomai** is a "participle"—meaning though it appears as a verb, it will function (typically) as a noun or adjective. Young's Literal Translation renders it: "at the coming of the Holy Spirit upon you."

6.1.6–As we examined, the historical event of Pentecost, which Jesus promised with the coming of the Holy Spirit, was in the future for the disciples (between 7–10 days). Yet, we can look at the historical context of this event and better understand what Jesus refers to.

- Pentecost comes from the Greek word **pentēkostē**, meaning "fiftieth" (fifty days after Passover)

- What can you discover about Pentecost from Acts 2:1–4 and Peter's explanation of what happened (see Acts 2:5–47)?

- What else is this event called? (see Luke 24:49; Acts 1:4; 2:33)

- How does the giving of the Holy Spirit at Pentecost compare to and fulfill the first Pentecost (also called the Feast of Weeks or the Feast of Harvest… celebrating the giving of the Law)? See Exodus 19:16–20; 23:16; 32:28; 34:22–23; Leviticus 23:15–21; Deuteronomy 4:10–13; 16:16–17.

6.1.7–The geographical context is a primary focus in this passage. Jesus refers to four key geographical locations. See what you can discover about each (biblically and geographically), how they are related, and consider what significance these four locations have in the context of Jesus talking with His disciples. Consider using an online Bible dictionary (like blueletterbible.org) and atlas.

- Jerusalem

- Judea

- Samaria

- Ends of the Earth

6.1.8–Are there any other observations, questions, or insights you can glean from our passage? Consider using the "what to look fors" list in Appendix 5.

6.1.9–After making your list of observations, it is sometimes helpful to consult commentaries and other Bible resources to see if there are any additional insights you missed or ideas that spark more observations. Resources can also help you find answers to unresolved questions.

Remember that commentaries are not Scripture, and you need to be discerning while reading them; as such, it can help to use resources from multiple theological perspectives so you can wrestle with the text and come to a conclusion yourself.

Consider examining several free commentaries on Acts 1:8 in an online resource (like blueletterbible.org).

I've also given several quotations below from other commentaries I've paid for (in no particular order). Highlight or summarize your discoveries.

> The locations mentioned in this verse represent a geographical broadening in scope of the apostles' mission, from Israel's capital, to the land of Israel, and to the entire world. This also reflects the structure of the book of Acts: The Church spreads in Jerusalem (chs. 1–7), in Judaea and Samaria (ch. 8), and to the surrounding nations (chs. 9–28). Compare Isa 49:6.[38]

> An Old Testament prophet had called the people of Israel to be God's witnesses in the world (Isa. 43:10; 44:8); the task which Israel had not fulfilled was taken on by Jesus, the perfect Servant of the Lord, and shared by him with his disciples. The close relation between God's call to Israel, "you are my witnesses," and the risen Lord's commission to his apostles, "you will be my witnesses," can be appreciated the more if we consider the implications of Paul's quotation of Isa. 49:6 in Acts 13:47. There the heralds of the gospel are spoken of as a light for the Gentiles, bearing God's salvation "to the end of the earth"; here "the end of the earth" and nothing short of that is to be the limit of the apostolic witness.[39]

> *you will be witnesses to me.* This statement sums up the main theme of Acts; the apostles are to give testimony to all peoples about what Jesus "did and taught" (1:1), in effect, about the Word of God that he preached: "In his name repentance for the forgiveness of sins shall be preached to all the nations—beginning from Jerusalem! You are witnesses of this!" (Luke 24:47–48). It must now spread abroad through such testimony borne by Jesus' followers, first of all by apostles, but then by others; they are all to become ministers of the

Word, empowered by his Spirit. Testimony thus becomes a literary theme in Acts, reappearing in 1:22; 2:32; 3:15; 4:20, 33; 5:32; 8:25; 10:39, 41; 13:31; 18:5; 20:21, 24; 22:15, 18, 20; 23:11; 26:16; 28:23.[40]

The sphere of the apostolic witness was to be 'in Jerusalem, and in all Judea and Samaria, and to the ends of the earth'. Jesus echoes the words and concepts of Isaiah 49:6, especially with the phrase to the ends of the earth. 'Rather than sinking roots in Jerusalem and waiting for the world to flood in, Jesus' followers are to move out from Jerusalem, through Judea and Samaria, and ultimately "to the ends of the earth".' More of this text is quoted in Acts 13:47, as a justification for Paul's ministry among the Gentiles, and it is alluded to in Luke 2:32; Acts 26:23, and possibly 28:28. 'The promise of God's reign is not simply the restoration of the preserved of Israel, but the renewal of the vocation of Israel to be a light to the nations to the ends of the earth.' Acts 1:8 is a prediction and promise of the way this divine plan will be fulfilled, rather than a command. The rest of the book shows how it happened, first in Jerusalem (chap. 2–7), then in all Judea and Samaria (chap. 8–12), and then to the ends of the earth (chap. 13–28). However, Rome is not the ultimate goal of this mission, even though Acts finishes with Paul's ministry in that city.[41]

Jewish people often viewed Jerusalem as the world's center; Luke's first volume begins and ends there, but his second volume progresses from Jerusalem to Rome. Many in Luke's world thought of Spain as the western end of the earth, Ethiopia (8:27; cf. Lk 11:31) as the southern end, and knew of the east as far as China. Although Acts climaxes with the gospel reaching the heart of the empire, Luke's immediate world, "the ends of the earth" looks beyond this to all peoples (e.g., Isa 45:22; 52:10).[42]

One of the great gifts of Pentecost is that all believers can now speak for God (2:14–21). In a sense all believers are prophets. No believer is a mere fan but a player! The apostles certainly led the church, but the gospel advanced largely through the words and deeds of unordained and uneducated people — informal missionaries. The church today, in fact, desperately needs to recover this practice. The only difference in a believer sitting in his or her American home and a foreign missionary on the field is location, not identity. Every Christian is a missionary. And so each of us should ask, Where do I serve? To whom do I minister?[43]

The first element of the risen Lord's promise is 'you will receive power' (*lēmpsesthe dynamin*), and the qualifying clause explains that this will happen 'when the Holy Spirit comes on you' (*epelthontos tou hagious pneumatos eph' hymas*; cf. Lk. 24:49). The Holy Spirit's 'coming' is not continuous but definitive (the context so delimits the aorist participle *epelthontos* to show that the meaning is temporal and punctiliar here), though clearly the Spirit is available at any time after Pentecost for those who repent and are 'baptized in the name of Jesus Christ' (2:38). In the light of v. 5, this coming of the Spirit upon the apostles must be equivalent to being baptized with the Holy Spirit (cf. 2:4 note).[44]

6.2 – WHAT DID THE PASSAGE MEAN TO THE ORIGINAL AUDIENCE? (INTERPRETATION)

So what? This is the time when we consider the interpretation of the passage. How do we understand all our observations in light of the original audience?

Go back and reread your observations, questions, and discoveries. Consider them in light of the context of Jesus giving His final words to His disciples prior to

His ascension. What was Jesus telling the disciples, and how would they have understood what He said?

Write out a summary of what the passage meant to the original audience. What is the key concept ("truth nugget")?

6.3 – HOW DOES THE INTERPRETATION CONNECT WITH THE REST OF SCRIPTURE? (CONNECTION)

Take the main concept you summarized in 6.2 and ask these three questions:

1. Are there any verses in Scripture that seem to contradict the main concept of the passage I am studying? If so, how do I reconcile my understanding of Acts 1:8 with those passages?

2. Are there any verses that can help refine my understanding of the passage I am studying? Cross-references are sometimes helpful for this.

3. How is this concept expressed, illustrated, or expanded in both the Old and New Testaments?

6.4 – WHAT DOES IT CHANGE IN MY LIFE? (APPLICATION)

As mentioned, we must apply the truth of God's Word to our lives if we want to be changed. Look back at the summary of your key concept. How can you apply the truth principle to your life? Here are some key questions to consider — don't be general; the more specific you are, the better.

- So what? What does it change in my life?

- What specific changes need to happen for me to live and apply this passage in my life?

- How does this concept apply personally to my life (my emotions, marriage, work, free time, family, thought life, etc.)?

- How will I obey and bring about those changes (by God's grace and enablement)?

- What is the one verse to commit to memory (that sums up the concept of the passage I studied)?

- What illustration can I create to remind me of the passage and the concept?

- How can I take this passage and concept and turn it into a personal prayer of surrender unto God?

Before and after you ask the questions, spend time in prayer and ask God:

- to reveal and teach you how you can apply the truth to your life

- to give you the grace to obey

- to busy His Word in your heart and enable it to bear fruit

- to take the information of His Word and allow it to radically transform your life

GUIDED TOPICAL STUDY

Humility

We will take the nine-step path mentioned in chapter 14 and examine what the Bible says on the topic of humility. Remember, there is no rush. Take your time throughout the study to think, review, and reflect upon the topic.

———————

For a printable version of this guided study, visit **deeperChristian.com/saturationbook**.

———————

1. CHOOSE A TOPIC

Humility.

2. PRAY

Before you engage in the Word, ask the Holy Spirit

to give you insight, wisdom, and understanding into His Word.

Take the time before every study to:

- Consecrate your heart and mind

- Surrender your life and will

- Ask for wisdom, insight, and grace to understand

- Commit to obey His Word regardless of how difficult it may be

- Declare that you desire to know Him (not just information) and that you long for the Word to sanctify and transform your life so that you might be conformed to the image of Christ

- Ask for His involvement, grace, and enablement not only in the study but to live it out

3. WHAT DO YOU ALREADY KNOW? WHAT ASSUMPTIONS ARE YOU MAKING?

Before we look at what Scripture says about humility, what do you already know? What assumptions do you come to the topic with? Write down everything you can think of about humility and what you remember Scripture saying about it.

4. LOOK IT UP AND WRITE IT DOWN

One of the best ways to start a topic study is to use a concordance to look up words, phrases, and synonyms for your topic.

4A. MAKE A LIST OF VERSES

Go to an online resource like blueletterbible.org and type in words for humility (humility, humble, lowliness, meekness, etc.). Make a list of all the verses you find with the concept of humility.

Because Hebrew and Greek words can have several English translations, it is often helpful to find a key passage in the Old and New Testaments and look up what the Hebrew or Greek word is, how it is translated, and where else in Scripture that word is used.

For an example of how to do this in blueletterbible, please visit **deeperChristian.com/saturationbook**.

4B. READ AND MAKE OBSERVATIONS

Read through the verses you found and make a list of insights, thoughts, and summaries of what you discover. Remember to read the verses in their context (the surrounding passages).

For example, Philippians 2:3–4 says, "Do nothing from selfishness or empty conceit, but with humility of mind regard one another as more important than yourselves; do not merely look out for your own personal interests, but also for the interests of others." A few simple observations we can make are:

- Nothing in our lives should be done from selfishness or "empty conceit" (also translated as "vainglory" or "trying to impress others" — i.e., pride).

- A key aspect of humility is to regard one another as more important than oneself.

- Another key aspect of humility is to be more interested in the needs of others than my own.

4C. WORD STUDIES

Understanding the topic in its original context is important. Go back and find a few key passages, look up the word, and discover what it means.

To help you work through some of the keywords, here is what one Bible resource says about the different terms used for humility in Scripture:

> In the OT, Hebrew ענע ('nh) carries the basic sense of "to crouch" or "to bend low to the ground"—either to express submissiveness or to metaphorically describe one's impoverished condition. Some forms of the verb עָנָה ('ānâ) signify being made low or humble by outside forces, while other forms signify humiliating other people. The nouns עָנָו ('ānāw, "bowed, afflicted, humble") and עֲנָוָה ('ānāwâ, "humility") refer to humble or meek conditions. There is also a related adjective עָנִי ('ānî, "poor, afflicted, humble"), which has a wide range of applications—spiritual, physical, and mental.
> Several words in the Greek NT convey the idea of humility or modesty of character. There is a key family of related words: the adjectives ταπεινός (tapeinos; "lowly, humble") and ταπεινόφρων (tapeinophrōn; "humble"), the verb ταπεινόω (tapeinoō; "to humble, lower"), and the nouns ταπεινοφροσύνη (tapeinophrosynē; "humility") and ταπείνωσις (tapeinōsis, "humiliation"). Most of these terms may carry spiritual or physical connotations. Additionally, when the Greek word μικρός (micros, "small, little") is used in a spiritual sense, it refers to a state of humility.[45]

Do your own word studies on a few of the main words used until you have a good understanding of what humility means, based on the definition and on where it is used in Scripture.

4D. EXAMINE THE OPPOSITE

In studying a topic, it is also helpful to consider examining passages that talk about the opposite of the topic — in our study, it would be pride and selfishness. Do a basic search and write down what the Bible says about pride.

Make sure you examine: Psalm 5:1–12; Proverbs 16:18–19; Jeremiah 9:23–24; Matthew 23:1–36; Luke 18:9–14; Romans 1:18–2:24; 12:9–21; 1 Corinthians 1:26–31; 13:1–13; 2 Timothy 3:1–9; Titus 1:5–9; James 3:1–4:17; 1 Peter 5:5–11; 2 Peter 2:4–11 (especially in light of Ezekiel 16:49–50); 1 John 2:15–17.

What do these verses and others you found on pride help you understand our topic of humility?

5. SUMMARIZE CONCEPTS AND PRINCIPLES

Organize and summarize your study into central concepts and principles. What sub-themes does the Bible give for humility?

For example, you may want to organize your passages and insights based on how the Bible defines humility, how to live it, how Jesus lived and demonstrated humility, the blessings if you are humble, and the warning against those who don't.

However you organize the material, read through and group your insights together so you can see patterns, emphasis, etc. Note: this is easier to do digitally as you can copy and paste your findings into concepts and themes.

Once finished, go back and summarize each of the concepts and sub-themes for quick reference.

For example, as an overarching summary of what I've discovered so far in Scripture, humility is not about personality, quietness, or thinking I have little value. Instead it has more to do with getting my mind off myself. Pride, the opposite of humility, is about self-focus, self-accomplishment, self, self, self. So to walk in humility doesn't mean I lack value (Jesus bought me with a price), but it does mean I stop focusing on myself. I embrace and clothe myself with humility (see 1 Peter 5:5) while allowing the Spirit of God to do a transformative work in my life so that I quit worrying about what others think and be willing to take the lowest place. Humility is about keeping my focus on Christ and seeing myself in light of Him and the standard He has called me to in His Word — in short, I desperately need Jesus and His grace in my life.

6. ASK QUESTIONS AND KEEP WRESTLING

Though we have organized the material, are there any lingering questions you have on humility? Are there any passages of Scripture that appear to challenge or contradict what you are discovering about humility? Search Scripture and wrestle with any questions or tensions and come to a biblical conclusion.

7. CLARIFY AND SIMPLIFY

Define and summarize the topic of humility as simply as possible in a single paragraph (preferably no more than a page).

To take this a step further, consider reducing the summary paragraph into a concise sentence that gives the fundamental concept. How would you explain the topic to someone if you only had one sentence?

8. CHECK

Before you finish, consider exploring the topic of humility in a Bible dictionary or other Bible resource to "check your work" and give additional insights you may have missed. If your understanding of humility is vastly different from the resource, go back and re-examine the topic. If there are slight differences, use the resource to help push back on your study and think it through on another level.

Remember, we are not trying to prove our point or preference. Instead, we desire to know what God's Word says on humility so we can submit our understanding and lives to His truth.

Here are a few helpful insights from resources I examined.

HOLMAN ILLUSTRATED BIBLE DICTIONARY

HUMILITY The personal quality of being free from arrogance and pride and having an accurate estimate of one's worth.

Old Testament The OT connects the quality of humility with Israel's lowly experience as slaves in Egypt — a poor, afflicted, and suffering people (Deut. 26:6). The Hebrew word translated as humility is similar to another Hebrew word meaning "to be afflicted." In OT thought, humility was closely associated with individuals who were poor and afflicted (2 Sam. 22:28). What God desires most is not outward sacrifices but a humble spirit (Ps. 51:17; Mic. 6:8). Such a humble spirit shows itself in several ways: a recognition of one's sinfulness before a holy God (Isa. 6:5), obedience to God (Deut. 8:2), and submission to God (2 Kings 22:19; 2 Chron. 34:27).

The OT promised blessings to those who were humble: wisdom (Prov. 11:2), good tidings (Isa. 61:1), and honor (Prov. 15:33).

The experience of many kings indicated that those who humble themselves before God will be exalted (1 Kings 21:29; 2 Kings 22:19; 2 Chron. 32:26; 33:12–19). Those who do not humble themselves before God will be afflicted (2 Chron. 33:23; 36:12). The pathway to revival is the way of humility (2 Chron. 7:14).

New Testament Jesus Christ's life provides the best example of what it means to have humility (Matt. 11:29; 1 Cor. 4:21; Phil. 2:1–11). Jesus preached and taught often about the need for humility (Matt. 23:12; Mark 9:35; Luke 14:11; 18:14). He urged those who desired to live by kingdom standards to practice humility (Matt. 18:1; 23:12).

The person with humility does not look down on others (Matt. 18:4; Luke 14:11). Humility in the NT is closely connected with the quality of gentleness (Matt. 5:5). While God resists those who are proud, He provides grace for the humble (James 4:6). Primary in the NT is the conviction that one who has humility will not be overly concerned about his or her prestige (Matt. 18:4; 23:12; Rom. 12:16; 2 Cor. 11:7).

Paul believed that quality relationships with other people, especially those who had erred spiritually, hinged on the presence of gentleness or humility (1 Cor. 4:21; Gal. 6:1; 2 Tim. 2:25). The NT affirms, as does the OT, that God will exalt those who are humble and bring low those who are proud (Luke 1:52; James 4:10; 1 Pet. 5:6). The Greek world abhorred the quality of gentleness or humility, but the Christian community believed these qualities were worthy (2 Cor. 10:18; Col. 3:12; Eph. 4:2).[46]

EASTON'S BIBLE DICTIONARY

[Humility is] a prominent Christian grace (Rom. 12:3; 15:17, 18; 1 Cor. 3:5–7; 2 Cor. 3:5; Phil. 4:11–13). It is a state of mind well pleasing to God (1 Pet. 3:4); it preserves the soul in tranquillity (Ps. 69:32, 33), and makes us patient under trials (Job 1:22).

Christ has set us an example of humility (Phil. 2:6–8). We should be led thereto by a remembrance of our sins (Lam. 3:39), and by the thought that it is the way to honour (Prov. 16:18), and that the greatest promises are made to the humble (Ps. 147:6; Isa. 57:15; 66:2; 1 Pet. 5:5). It is a "great paradox in Christianity that it makes humility the avenue to glory."[47]

ZONDERVAN ILLUSTRATED BIBLE DICTIONARY

The concept of humility shades off in various directions, but the central thought is freedom from pride — lowliness, meekness, modesty, mildness. There is a "false humility" (Col. 2:18, 23; NRSV, "self-abasement"). God humbles people to bring them to obedience (Deut. 8:2). To humble ourselves is a condition of God's favor (2 Chr. 7:14) and his supreme requirement (Mic. 6:8). God dwells with the humble (Isa. 57:15). Humility is encouraged (Prov. 15:33; 18:12; 22:4). To the Greeks humility was weak and despicable, but Jesus made it the cornerstone of character (Matt. 5:3, 5; 18:4; 23:12; Lk. 14:11; 18:14). Jesus by his humility drew people to himself (Matt. 11:28–30; Jn. 13:1–20; Rev. 3:20). PAUL emphasized the humility of Jesus (2 Cor. 8:9; Phil. 2:1–11), commanded us to be humble toward one another (Rom. 12:10; 1 Cor. 13:4–6; Phil. 2:3–4), and spoke of himself as an example (Acts 20:19). PETER exhorted humility before the brethren and before God (1 Pet. 5:5–6).[48]

DICTIONARY OF BIBLICAL IMAGERY

The terminology for humility appears nearly a hundred times in the Bible, referencing multiple meanings. Humility reflects godly character (Ps 45:4) — even Jesus was humble (Mt 11:29). It is also associated with wisdom (Prov 11:2; Jas 3:13) and meekness (Job 8:7; Zeph 3:12). Paradoxically, the humble deserve honor (Prov 15:33; 18:12) and the humbled will be exalted (Mt 23:12; also Lk 14:11).

The humble are known for their fear of the Lord (Prov 22:4) and their righteousness (Num 12:3; Zeph 2:3; Acts 20:19; Phil 2:3), but false humility comes from the ungodly, who have no place in heaven (Col 2:18, 23). Believers are commanded to assume humility before everyone (Phil 2:3; Titus 3:2) and especially to humble themselves before God (Ex 10:3; Prov 6:3; Mt 18:4; Jas 4:10). They are even to be clothed with humility (Col 3:12; 1 Pet 5:5). Often humility comes in the form of testing or discipline (Deut 8:2; 1 Kings 11:39).

Humility is always the proper posture before God and others; by contrast, humiliation is never seen as a virtue in Scripture. On the contrary, it is often a punishment brought on by God (Mal 2:9; Lk 13:17) or one's own doing (Prov 25:7; Lk 14:9). Humiliating others is a sin (1 Cor 11:22).[49]

LEXHAM THEOLOGICAL WORDBOOK

In both the OT and NT, humility is important for establishing a proper relationship with God, with others, and with oneself (e.g., Prov 22:4; Jas 4:10). The act of bowing low to the ground expresses submissiveness and thus is associated with the virtue of humility. Humility is often listed with righteousness to portray a more complete image of the essential virtues (e.g., Psa 45:4). Humility before God can be expressed through fasting (Lev 23:29).

The prophet Zechariah presents the coming Messiah King as humble (Zech 9:9; Matt 21:4–5). In the great invitation, Jesus characterizes himself as gentle and humble (tapeinos) in order to encourage others to come to him (Matt 11:27–29). Jesus demonstrates his humility by submitting to the Father's will, especially in the garden of Gethsemane, where he prayed that the Father's will be done (e.g., Luke 22:40–46). The ultimate act of humility is Christ's submission to the crucifixion (Phil 2:6–8); his humility serves as an example for every Christian to emulate (Phil 2:1–5).

Humility as a state of being appears in a variety of ways. Individuals or nations may be humbled or afflicted by God as a punishment for sin (e.g., Deut 8:2; 1 Kgs 8:35) or as an encouragement for spiritual development (Psa 119:71). Humility may involve unfavorable conditions characterized by afflictions (Psa 119:107), poverty (Jas 1:9), or even imprisonment (Judg 16:5–19). Humility therefore has both positive and negative connotations. On one hand, a humble spirit produced by divine action, by one's initiative, or by another's action may be a profitable and enriching condition, but on the other hand, consequences that one may experience by oppressive powers, by the sinful actions of others, or by difficult social conditions may be more humiliating than helpful.[50]

9. APPLY

I've repeatedly stated that Bible study is not for information but for transformation. When you finish your study, spend time and allow the Holy Spirit to examine your life and reveal any area that needs to change. Don't merely esteem the Word, be changed by it (see John 17:17).

According to Scripture, can your life be described as "humble"? If not, what needs to change? How can you walk in greater humility today?

ENDNOTES

1   Elisabeth Elliott, ed., *The Journals of Jim Elliot* (Old Tappan, NJ: Fleming H. Revell, 1978), 309.

2   Or perhaps Jesus mentioned some of my other favorites:

  · The only begotten son given to be our provision (Genesis 22)

  · The Heavenly Tabernacle come to dwell among us (Exodus 25:8–9, Revelation 21:3)

  · The ark of our redemption and our covering for sin (Exodus 25:10–22)

  · Our refuge and hiding place (Numbers 35; Psalm 7:1)

  · The Kinsman Redeemer (Ruth)

  · The Good Shepherd (Psalm 23, John 10)

  · The Branch (Isaiah 4:2; Jeremiah 23:5; 33:15; Zechariah 3:8; 6:12)

  · The Mediator of the New Covenant (Jeremiah 31:31–33)

3   It is interesting to note that while the Apostle Peter walked physically with Jesus and heard God's voice from heaven (see Matthew 17:5; 2 Peter 1:17–18), he still said that Scripture is "the prophetic word made more sure, to which you do well to pay attention as to a lamp shining in a dark place…" (2 Peter 1:19). According to Peter, it is the unchanging Word of God which is to be the sure foundation of our lives. No dream, vision, prophetic

insight, sermon, or anything else is on the same level as the authority of Scripture itself. We must be Bereans (see Acts 17:11) and discern (test) everything against the perfect standard of God's Word.

4 Martin Luther, *Comments on Psalm 90; Concordia Triglotta (F. C. II, 20–21)*, (Wauwatosa, WI: Northwestern Publishing House, 1996), 889.

5 George Whitefield, *Sermons on Important Subjects* (London: Thomas Tegg, 1841), 50.

6 Ian Thomas, *The Saving Life of Christ and The Mystery of Godliness* (Grand Rapids, MI: Zondervan, 1988), 186.

7 For note, though Scripture has tensions, nothing contradicts. Modern culture has accused the Bible of having countless contradictions and errors, yet we know God's Word is true, and as the very words of God, there are no contradictions. If you find what you think is a tension or contradiction, if you labor to understand the passages, you always find greater truth and insight. While I don't understand everything in Scripture, I've never found a single contradiction despite thousands of hours of study.

8 A.W. Tozer, *Experiencing the Presence of God: Teachings from the Book of Hebrews*, ed. James L. Snyder (Ventura, CA: Regal, 2010), 44.

9 Kay Arthur, *The New How to Study Your Bible* (Eugene, OR: Harvest House, 2010, page 10).

10 https://www.thattheworldmayknow.com/green-pastures (accessed May 18, 2022).

11 For more details on the inspiration and authority of Scripture, see Appendix 2.

12 Author unknown.

13 Bill Mounce, https://www.billmounce.com/bible-study-greek/was-timothy-pauls-legitimate-or-spiritual-son-1-tim-1-2 (accessed April 30, 2022).

14 Mark L. Strauss, *BI181 Introducing Bible Translations*, Logos Mobile Education (Bellingham, WA: Lexham Press,

2014). Mark goes on to explain that translation is a two-step process:

- It follows that all translation is interpretation. Every word, every phrase, every idiom must first be interpreted—in other words, its meaning must first be understood before it can be translated. How would you say it, then, in the receptor language, or the target language?

  So translation is always a two-step process. Translators must first exegete the text. They must first interpret it and understand what the text meant in its original context—its literary context (the words around it), [and] its historical context (what these phrases meant in that particular time and place).

  Once the text is accurately interpreted and understood, the translator has to ask the next question: How is this meaning best expressed? How it is best conveyed in the receptor language, or in that target language? So translation is always more than a simple replacement of words—and since all translation is interpretation, no translation can be perfect. As we said, something is always lost in the translation, and that is certainly true.

15 To learn more about the genres and literature of the Bible, see Howard & William Hendricks's book *Living By the Book*, chapter 29; and Leland Ryken's book *How to Read the Bible as Literature* and his *Reading the Bible as Literature* series.

16 Chiasms appear all throughout Scripture, not just in the Psalms. The typical structure is like a sandwich where you have parallel lines that repeat, echo, or explain each other as it builds to a key focal point in the passage. For example, Proverbs 6:16–19 tells us:

There are six things which the LORD hates, yes, seven which are an abomination to Him:

1a) Haughty eyes,
 2a) a lying tongue,
   3a) And hands that shed innocent blood,
     KEY FOCUS) A heart that devises
       wicked plans,
   3b) Feet that run rapidly to evil,
  2b) A false witness who utters lies,
1b) And one who spreads [sows] strife among brothers.

Notice how 1a and 1b expand on each other (the same haughty nature that is full of arrogance and disdain is the same that spreads strife). 2a (lying tongue) and 2b (uttering lies and a false witness) parallel each other. 3a and 3b deal with hands and feet. The focal point of the passage summarizes each line: a heart that devises wicked plans—pride, lies, and evil are produced from a wicked heart. And these are all things God hates. For a list of other Bible chiasms, check out the bonus resources for this book at deeperChristian.com/saturationbook.

17 Image courtesy of Bill Welch. Lightstock.com/128870.

18 Author unknown.

19 Sometimes the truth is found in the tension. For example (to step on a bunch of theological toes), is God sovereign or does He give man free will? The answer is yes to both. To go to either extreme demands you ignore certain Scriptures or create elaborate theological explanations. What if the Bible means what it says? Rather than attempting to interpret the Bible based on a theological position, what if (again) we come humbly and honestly to the text? The Bible declares that God is both sovereign and, strangely enough, gives us free will. If man didn't have free will then God is a puppet master responsible for everything, including my sin—which is not true since He is not an author of sin nor does any sin reside within Him. Yet to ignore His sovereignty perverts His nature and grace. So to remain biblical, we must rest in the tension that God is both sovereign and gives humans free will. Holding this truth in tension actually increases His sovereignty. As we recognize and wrestle with the tensions of Scripture, we begin to more deeply understand the richness, beauty, and brilliance of our God and His Word. A few other major tensions as examples:

- God's love and God's wrath

- God is One yet Triune

- Faith and works in the Christian life (see the writings of Paul and James)

- Israel as God's chosen people and Christians as the people of God

- The Kingdom of God as "now" and "not yet"

- God's unconditional faithfulness, mercy, and love and His conditional commands (if… then)

20 Author unknown.

21 State of the Bible 2022, American Bible Society, pages 16–17.

22 Elisabeth Elliott, ed., *The Journals of Jim Elliot* (Old Tappan, NJ: Fleming H. Revell, 1978), 309.

23 F. F. Bruce, *The Books and the Parchments, rev. ed.* (Westwood, N.J.: Fleming H. Revell, 1963), 88.

24 I am indebted to Tim Mackey of the Bible Project for the term "Jewish meditation literature." For more on this idea and see several examples of major themes and threads of thought that become apparent upon multiple readings of Scripture, see the bonus resources for this book at: deeperChristian.com/saturationbook.

25 W. T. Purkiser, *Exploring the Old Testament* (Kansas City, MO: Beacon Hill Press, 1955), 48–49.

26 Wayne Grudem, *Systematic Theology: An Introduction to Biblical Doctrine, Second Edition.* (Grand Rapids, MI: Zondervan Academic, 2020), 85.

27 Rob Bell, *Velvet Elvis* (Grand Rapids: Zondervan, 2005), 22, 27.

28 John Wesley, *Sermons, on Several Occasions* (Oak Harbor, WA: Logos Research Systems, Inc., 1999), preface.

29 If you are interested in understanding the difference between a word-for-word translation and a paraphrase (and why you should study from a word-for-word translation), I have an article you can read at: deeperChristian.com/saturationbook.

30 M. G. Easton, *Illustrated Bible Dictionary and Treasury of Biblical History, Biography, Geography, Doctrine, and Literature* (New York: Harper & Brothers, 1893), 149.

31 James Newell, "Cistern," ed. Chad Brand et al., *Holman Illustrated Bible Dictionary* (Nashville, TN: Holman Bible Publishers, 2003), 300–301.

32 Bruce Wilkinson and Kenneth Boa, *Talk Thru the Bible* (Nashville, TN: Thomas Nelson, 1983), 327, 352.

33 Stephen Manley, *Acts 1 Commentary* (Lebanon, TN: Cross Style Press, 2015), 3–4.

34 Here is my outline of our passage. Yours likely will look different but have a good reason for why you divided the passage as you did, or go back and reconsider your divison points.
  1:1–3   The Introduction
  1:4–8   The Commission
  1:9-11   The Ascension

35 Matthew Henry, *Matthew Henry's Commentary on the Whole Bible: Complete and Unabridged in One Volume* (Peabody: Hendrickson, 1994), 2063.

36 James M. Hamilton Jr. and Brian J. Vickers, *John–Acts*, ed. Iain M. Duguid, James M. Hamilton Jr., and Jay Sklar, vol. IX, *ESV Expository Commentary* (Wheaton, IL: Crossway, 2019), 337.

37 Clinton E. Arnold, *Acts*, ed. Clinton E. Arnold, vol. 2B, *Zondervan Illustrated Bible Backgrounds Commentary* (Grand Rapids, MI: Zondervan, 2002), 9.

38 John D. Barry et al., *Faithlife Study Bible* (Bellingham, WA: Lexham Press, 2012, 2016), Ac 1:8.

39 F. F. Bruce, *The Book of the Acts, The New International Commentary on the New Testament* (Grand Rapids, MI: Wm. B. Eerdmans Publishing Co., 1988), 36.

40 Joseph A. Fitzmyer, *The Acts of the Apostles: A New Translation with Introduction and Commentary, vol. 31, Anchor Yale Bible* (New Haven; London: Yale University Press, 2008), 206.

41 David G. Peterson, *The Acts of the Apostles, The Pillar New Testament Commentary* (Grand Rapids, MI; Nottingham, England: William B. Eerdmans Publishing Company, 2009), 112.

42 Craig S. Keener and John H. Walton, eds., *NIV Cultural Backgrounds Study Bible: Bringing to Life the Ancient World of Scripture* (Grand Rapids, MI: Zondervan, 2016), 1867.

43 Tony Merida, *Exalting Jesus in Acts* (Nashville, TN: Holman Reference, 2017), 10–11.

44 David G. Peterson, *The Acts of the Apostles, The Pillar New Testament Commentary* (Grand Rapids, MI; Nottingham, England: William B. Eerdmans Publishing Company, 2009), 110.

45 G. Scott Gleaves, "Humility," ed. Douglas Mangum et al., *Lexham Theological Wordbook, Lexham Bible Reference Series* (Bellingham, WA: Lexham Press, 2014).

46 Gary Hardin, "Humility," ed. Chad Brand et al., *Holman Illustrated Bible Dictionary* (Nashville, TN: Holman Bible Publishers, 2003), 792–793.

47 M. G. Easton, *Illustrated Bible Dictionary and Treasury of Biblical History, Biography, Geography, Doctrine, and Literature* (New York: Harper & Brothers, 1893), 340.

48 Moisés Silva, J. D. Douglas, and Merrill C. Tenney, eds., "Humility," *Zondervan Illustrated Bible Dictionary* (Grand Rapids, MI: Zondervan, 2011), 632.

49 Leland Ryken et al., *Dictionary of Biblical Imagery* (Downers Grove, IL: InterVarsity Press, 2000), 407.

50 G. Scott Gleaves, "Humility," ed. Douglas Mangum et al., *Lexham Theological Wordbook, Lexham Bible Reference Series* (Bellingham, WA: Lexham Press, 2014).